Global Imbalances and the Lessons of Bretton Woods

Global Imbalances and the Lessons of Bretton Woods

Barry Eichengreen

The Cairoli Lectures
Universidad Torcuato
Di Tella

The MIT Press
Cambridge, Massachusetts
London, England

MIT Press books may be purchased at special quantity discounts for business or sales promotional use. For information, please e-mail <special_sales@mitpress.mit.edu> or write to Special Sales Department, The MIT Press, 55 Hayward Street, Cambridge, MA 02142.

This book was set in Palatino by SPI Publishing Services. Printed and bound in the United States of America.

Library of Congress Cataloging-in-Publication Data

Eichengreen, Barry J.
    Global imbalances and the lessons of Bretton Woods / Barry Eichengreen.
        p. cm. — (Cairoli lecture series)
    Also available in electronic form.
    Includes bibliographical references and index.
    ISBN-13: 978-0-262-05084-5 (alk. paper)
    ISBN-10: 0-262-05084-6 (alk. paper)
    1. International finance. 2. United Nations Monetary and Financial Conference (1944: Bretton Woods, N.H.) I. Title. II. Series.

HG3881.E3465 2006
332'.042—dc22

2006044929

10 9 8 7 6 5 4 3 2 1

For Michelle, as always

Contents

Series Foreword

Ricardo Cairoli (1921–1998) was a successful businessman and a committed public official, who, throughout his career devoted himself to enhancing the well-being of Argentina's society. In 1991, he founded Capital Markets Argentina, one of the major independent investment corporations in the country, offering services in brokerage and asset management. Since its inception, the corporation has been involved in numerous philanthropic activities. Currently his wife, Mrs. Haydee Morteo de Cairoli, and his children, Graciela and Pablo, continue to support higher education, sponsoring, among other initiatives, the Capital Markets Corporation Conferences in Business Economics. The conferences are organized by the Universidad Torcuato Di Tella, a private university founded in 1991, which rapidly established itself as a center of excellence for education and research in the social sciences in Latin America. The realization and publication of the conference lectures represents the joint commitment of Capital Markets Argentina and the Universidad Torcuato Di Tella to the advancement of knowledge.

Preface

The big message of this little book is that history must be read carefully for its policy implications. I take as my foil a series of articles by Michael Dooley, David Folkerts-Landau, and Peter Garber, three authors who have influentially used the history of the Bretton Woods international monetary system that operated from the late 1950s through the early 1970s to make some points about the operation of today's international financial system. Then as now, according to Dooley, Folkerts-Landau, and Garber, the United States occupied an asymmetric position at the center of the international system, running balance-of-payments deficits, providing international reserves to other countries, and acting as export market of last resort for the rest of the world. Other countries kept their currencies pegged to the dollar. They were reluctant to revalue even in the face of chronic American balance-of-payments deficits and even where they enjoyed relatively rapid productivity growth for fear of interrupting the process of export-led growth and suffering capital

losses on their foreign reserves. The original Bretton
Woods system, based on these structural factors, endured
for many years. The implication is that the new informal
Bretton Woods system that has developed spontaneously
in recent years is likely to prove equally durable. To put it
another way, since structural factors underlie the current
pattern of exchange rates (undervalued Asian currencies
and an overvalued dollar) and global imbalances (Asian
surpluses and U.S. deficits), this situation is likely to
endure for a considerable time to come.

As always, the closer one examines a history, the more
complicated it appears. On closer scrutiny, important differences are apparent in the structure of today's world
economy compared to the 1960s. Taken together these factors point to the conclusion that the current constellation
of exchange rates and payments imbalances is unlikely to
persist for as long as the original Bretton Woods system.

A broad overview of these differences is provided in
chapter 1. Subsequent chapters then develop the contrasts
in more detail. Chapter 2 examines the Gold Pool, the collective agreement through which the central banks of
other advanced nations attempted to resist the temptation
to diversify their reserves out of dollars into gold and thus
to prevent their currencies from rising. It suggests that the
history of the Gold Pool is less than reassuring for those
who believe that contemporary central banks will continue to act collectively to support the dollar. Chapter 3
examines the case of Japan, a country that had long
pegged its currency to the American dollar and pursued a

policy of export-led growth but that revalued and then floated in 1971 to 1973. Its history suggests that it is possible for a rapidly growing, export-dependent economy to exit from a peg without killing the golden goose of growth and that differences between Japan then and China now make this potential scenario even more likely today. Chapter 4, finally, draws out the implications of the fact that today, unlike in the 1960s, there exists a full-fledged rival to the dollar in the form of the euro.

Each of these chapters illustrates the power of historical analogy in informing interpretations of current circumstances and future prospects. But the power of analogy resides not just in drawing out the parallels between two historical settings but also in highlighting the differences between them. It is those differences and their relatively pessimistic implications for the prospects for the dollar and the world economy that are emphasized in this book.

Earlier versions of these chapters were delivered as the Cairoli Lectures at the University Torcuato Di Tella in Buenos Aires. I thank Federico Sturzenegger for the invitation as well as for comments on the manuscript and Graciela Carioli and her family for supporting the lecture series. My friends in Argentina, including not only those in academia but also in the capital markets and at the central bank, created a stimulating atmosphere that enlivened my visit to Buenos Aires. Special thanks to Juan Pablo Nicolini, the rector at Di Tella, for doing much to ease my way.

Some of the chapters were tried out on other audiences at earlier dates. Chapter 1 was the basis of my Thornton Lecture to the Cass Business School at City University in London, while chapter 4 is a revision of my Tawney Lecture to the annual meetings of the Economic History Society in Leicester, England. I am grateful for the reactions of both audiences.

Chapter 3 was written jointly with Mariko Hatase of the Bank of Japan, who very graciously agreed to its inclusion here.[1] For help with sources, I thank Robert Solomon and Piet Clement. I also acknowledge permission to refer to materials from the U.S. National Archives, the Bank for International Settlements Archives, and the Public Record Office in London. At the MIT Press, Elizabeth Murry and her efficient staff made the transition from manuscript to book as painless as possible. I am grateful to them all.

History repeats itself, first as tragedy, then as farce.
—Karl Marx

History repeats itself; historians repeat each other.
—Philip Guedalla

Global Imbalances and the Lessons of Bretton Woods

1

Global Imbalances and the Lessons of Bretton Woods

An influential school of thought views the current international monetary and financial system as the Bretton Woods system reborn.[1] Today, as forty years ago, the international system is composed of core and peripheral economies. The core has the exorbitant privilege of issuing the currency used as international reserves and a tendency to live beyond its means. The periphery, which has a long way to go in catching up to the core, is committed to export-led growth based on the maintenance of an undervalued exchange rate, a corollary of which is its massive accumulation of low-yielding international reserves issued by and denominated in the currency of the center country. In the 1960s, the core was the United States and the periphery was Europe and Japan, the developing countries not yet having been fully integrated into the international system. Now, with the spread of globalization, there is a new periphery, the emerging markets of Asia, but the same old core, the United States, with the same tendency to live beyond its means.[2] The main difference between then and now, aside from the identities of the players, is the existence today of a third bloc, Europe, which has neither the periphery's scope for catch-up nor the reserve-currency country's ability to live beyond its means.

This contemporary view that a new, informal Bretton Woods–type system now exists yields strong predictions. It suggests that the current pattern of international settlements can be maintained, if not indefinitely then at least for an extended period. The United States can continue running current-account deficits because the emerging markets of Asia are anxious to accumulate additional international reserves in the form of dollars. There is no reason why the dollar must fall further, since there is no need for balance-of-payments adjustment; in particular, Asian countries are reluctant to see further appreciation of their currencies. The fact China has a rural population of 200 million underemployed workers still to be absorbed into the modern sector, something that it can do at the rate of only 10 million to 20 million a year, suggests that it will remain committed to its strategy of export-led growth for a decade and perhaps two. It follows that the current pattern of exchange rates and international payments can be maintained for at least as long.

This way of viewing the pattern of international settlements and the structure of the international monetary and financial system has much to recommend it. Among other things it encourages us to consider how national balances of payments fit together as interdependent elements of a larger international system. While systemic analyses were once commonplace in the literature on the international monetary and financial system, these have fallen out of fashion in recent years. Proponents of the new view are thus to be commended for reminding us that there is such a thing as the international monetary *system* and that the global balance of payments inclusive of reserve changes must sum to zero, something that should have implications for how we think about the world.

In addition, this new view helps us to understand how today's global imbalances arose in the first place. Developing countries, in Asia in particular, have long been committed to policies of export-led growth. Pegged exchange rates and a resistance to pressures for revaluation as their economies and current accounts strengthen have been at the center of their development strategies. In pursuing this approach, China is simply following in the footsteps of the newly industrializing economies of East Asia, which are following in the footsteps of Japan.[3] There is no question that their accumulation of reserves is a concomitant of intervention in the foreign-exchange market to keep their currencies down, which is in turn a corollary of the strategy of export-led growth. If this means lower incomes and living standards in the short run relative to those that could be achieved if currencies were allowed to appreciate, then this is fine so long as it translates into faster growth and even higher living standards down the road.

The analogy with the original Bretton Woods periphery, Europe and Japan in the 1950s and 1960s, is direct.

I myself have characterized the European social compact in this period as a willingness to trade wage restraint and accept lower levels of consumption in return for faster investment and export growth rates that promised significantly higher living standards down the road.[4] Others have emphasized the role of the same factors in the high-growth period in Japan.[5] Exchange rates that were increasingly undervalued as the period progressed were integral to this process.[6]

Moreover, there is no question that the United States plays a unique role in the international monetary and financial system today, just as it did forty years ago. It has been able to run current-account deficits without seeing the dollar fall significantly against the currencies of the periphery because the latter are concerned to preserve their position in the American market. This prompts central banks in the periphery to intervene with purchases of dollars to keep their exchange rates from appreciating. Their willingness to accumulate reserves is a consequence of the fact that their economies and trade are growing. It is reinforced by the lessons drawn from the emerging-market crises of the 1990s—namely, that the world is a risky place and that governments must insure against sudden shifts in financial flows by accumulating international reserves. And their willingness to accumulate reserves in the form of dollars reflects the exceptional depth and liquidity of the United States' financial markets, which makes it attractive for other countries to hold assets in this form.

In turn, these policies affect the incentive for the United States to adjust its policy mix. It feels less pressure to rein in public spending—to choose between guns and butter, in 1960s terminology—because the dollar-denominated securities that America is pumping into the world economy are happily absorbed by Asian central banks seeking to augment their reserves. The result is less dollar depreciation. Since the stimulus to demand applied by America's expansionary monetary and fiscal policies is matched by an increase in supply from China and other emerging markets, the result is less inflation. This means less pressure on the Federal Reserve to raise interest rates, relieving the central bank of the need to choose between price stability and growth- and employment-friendly monetary policies. Enjoying low funding costs, the government of the United States can have its cake and eat it too, boosting spending on both defense and social programs without having to resort to tax increases. In the rest of the world, preventing currencies from rising against the dollar means matching accommodative Federal Reserve policy dollar for dollar and basis point for basis point. The result is expanding credit aggregates and low real interest rates that show up first as "frothy" asset markets and eventually, some commentators fear, as accelerating inflation.[7]

So much for praise. I will now argue that this analogy and characterization of the Bretton Woods system are a misleading way of thinking about the prospects for the current international monetary and financial system. These analyses confuse the incentives that confronted individual countries under the original Bretton Woods system with the incentives that now confront groups of countries. They imagine the existence of a cohesive bloc of countries called *the periphery* that are ready and able to act in their collective interest. The idea that such a cartel existed in the 1960s is not entirely farfetched; it was called the Gold Pool.[8] But history shows that this cartel, like most cartels, proved impossible to hold together precisely when the need was greatest—that is, when collective action was needed for the maintenance of the system. The same point applies today: the Asian countries constituting the new periphery are similarly unlikely to be able to subordinate their individual interest to the collective interest.

The other way that this picture of a new Bretton Woods system misleads is that it underestimates how dramatically the world has changed. The members of the periphery are more numerous and heterogeneous today than they were in the 1960s. Then we were essentially talking about Europe and Japan. The countries of Europe had a common historical experience and had already begun constructing institutions to facilitate collective action and transnational governance. Japan, for unique historical reasons, was willing to provide support for the economic and financial policies of the United States to an unusual extent. By contrast, in Asia today supporting the United States is less of a priority. National stages of economic development and hence policy priorities are less uniform, which makes defining the collective interest more diffi-

cult. Moreover, regional cooperation is more weakly institutionalized than it was in Europe forty years ago. This
renders dubious the assumption that Asian countries will
work collectively to maintain the status quo.

Second, shifting out of dollars is only as attractive as
the next best alternative. By the mid-1960s, American
monetary gold reserves had fallen to barely half the $25
billion reached in the second half of the 1940s. Globally,
gold was in inelastic supply. The British pound sterling,
the second most important reserve currency, was hardly
an attractive alternative. Whether or not central banks
liked this situation, it lent stability to the prevailing international system. Now, in contrast, there is the euro.

Third, the readiness of foreign central banks to hold
dollars and the cohesiveness of their cartel depend on
their perception of the reserve-currency country's commitment to maintaining the value of their claims. Under
the Bretton Woods system, the United States accepted at
least a putative commitment to maintain the dollar's convertibility into gold at a fixed price. Now, in contrast, the
intentions of American policy makers are more obscure.
The prospects of the dollar's maintaining its value against
foreign currencies are also more dubious to the extent that
today fiscal deficits in the United States reflect the country's low savings rate, which does not bode well for the
sustainability of its debt at current price levels. This is
in contrast to the 1960s, when American capital outflows
reflected higher savings rates with more favorable implications for debt sustainability.

Fourth, the removal of capital controls makes it harder to bottle up private financial transactions that apply pressure to the current constellation of exchange rates. This forces central banks to undertake more extensive, costly, and difficult sterilization operations to maintain the status quo.

Fifth, the liberalization of domestic financial markets means that keeping the exchange rate low and domestic savings high no longer guarantees that additional investment will be centered in the traded-goods sector. In today's deregulated financial environment, there is a tendency for loose credit conditions to pump up investment in nontraded goods, notably real estate, fueling building booms and heightening financial fragility. Increasingly, Asian governments appreciate that the current strategy entails these risks, thus creating an incentive to modify it sooner rather than later.

The final point is that Asian policy makers are not unaware of this history. They understand that the world has changed in ways that diminish the attractions of systematic undervaluation designed to promote export-led growth. This makes it less likely that they will blindly repeat the policies of the past.

Back to the Future

The Bretton Woods system was a compromise between competing visions of the post–World War II monetary order. For the present expository purposes, it is sufficient to adopt the conventional distinction between the British and American views, although in reality there were a number of additional visions represented at the 1944 meeting convened in Bretton Woods, New Hampshire. The United States attached priority to stable monetary policy, an understandable goal given the turmoil that the country had endured in the 1930s. The British, in contrast, attached priority to their monetary freedom of action, again an understandable goal given how in the 1920s the Bank of England had been inhibited from adapting policy to the economy's needs. The compromise was one in which gold reserves were the ultimate anchor of the Bretton Woods system but subject to qualifications that enhanced the autonomy of central banks. The United States accepted, indeed embraced, the obligation of paying out gold at $35 an ounce. But this obligation was extended only to its official foreign creditors, not to private market participants.[9] And other currencies could be pegged to the dollar rather than to gold.

This first compromise was related to a second one mediating between the American desire for pegged exchange rates to promote the recovery of international trade and the British desire for exchange-rate adjustments to accommodate the policies necessary for the maintenance of internal balance. The result here was the awkwardly named *adjustable peg*, which was more adjustable in theory than in practice. Exchange rates could be changed, at least in principle, under carefully unspecified conditions.[10] This was what allowed Keynes in his famous speech to the House of

Lords to insist that the United Kingdom was not in fact tying itself to a new gold standard.[11]

In turn, that second compromise was related to a third—namely, between the American desire for currency convertibility and British insistence on the maintenance of controls. The result was a commitment to the early restoration of current account convertibility, which occurred in Europe at the end of 1959 and in Japan several years later, but combined with authorization to maintain controls on capital-account transactions for an indefinite period, which for some countries has meant up to the present day.

While the Bretton Woods system was nominally gold-based, from the start it was really a gold-dollar system. From 1968 with the creation of the two-tier gold market and especially from the summer of 1971 with the closure of the gold window, it was effectively a dollar standard. Given the inelasticity of global gold supplies, dollars provided essentially the entire increase over time in international reserves, other currencies playing a negligible role. The creation of Special Drawing Rights (SDRs) in 1968 came too late to change this fundamental fact, since the agreement took several years to implement and the first allocation of SDRs was issued only in 1970 to 1972.

While countries other than the United States could acquire additional reserves only if America ran balance-of-payments deficits, those deficits created discomfort for a number of reasons. Its status as the reserve-currency country allowed the United States to live beyond its means: the United States could import foreign merchandise, acquire foreign companies, and engage in foreign military adventures all at the same time. Charles de Gaulle and his political followers found these privileges particularly objectionable. Pressure on the dollar price of gold and official gold losses were a chronic preoccupation of American policy makers in the 1960s, but these pressures did nothing to assuage complaints that the United States had an "exorbitant privilege" by virtue of the dollar's exceptional position in the international financial system.[12]

Another reason that foreign central banks and governments were uncomfortable holding large stocks of dollar reserves was uncertainty about whether the dollar would maintain its value. If the dollar was devalued against gold or other currencies, foreign central banks would incur capital losses. If they sought to protect themselves by swapping their dollars for gold, they might precipitate the very crisis of which they were increasingly concerned. If the United States attempted to defend the dollar by adopting more restrictive monetary and fiscal policies or, more likely given domestic political imperatives, by resorting to protectionism to curtail the demand for imported merchandise, foreign economies would lose access to the export market on which they depended. These same considerations rendered foreign governments reluctant to revalue their currencies against the American dollar, despite their countries' relatively rapid growth, rising competitiveness, accretion of reserves, and reservations about the United States' balance-of-payments deficits.[13]

All this history has a remarkably contemporary ring. Then as now, other countries welcomed their ability to acquire dollar reserves and valued their access to a buoyant American export market. Then as now, they were reluctant to revalue for fear of how this would affect the prospects for export-led growth and the stability of the international monetary and financial system. Discerning no alternative, they resorted to a variety of ad hoc measures to keep the system running for more than a decade. One possible implication is that contemporary policy makers see no alternative to doing the same.

At the same time, the 1960s differed in important ways. In contrast to the current position, the United States' trade and current-account balances were in substantial *surplus* all through the period (see figure 1.1). Indeed, the American trade balance had been in surplus continuously since World War II. Similarly, its current account was in continuous surplus from 1954 to 1971, with the single exception of 1959. The United States' current account continued to strengthen through the first half of the 1960s until mounting American military expenditures abroad led to the progressive diminution of the surplus balance.[14] But a surplus there was.

Throughout the 1944 to 1973 period that dates the formal Bretton Woods system, then, the United States was a net investor abroad. Contemporaries were conscious of this fact. These were the years when critics in France and elsewhere became aware of the growing presence of American-based multinational corporations and worried

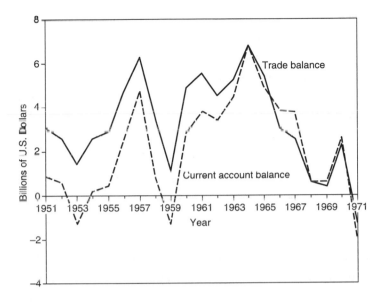

Figure 1.1
U.S. trade balance and current-account balance, 1951 to 1971
Source: U.S. President (1984).

that the United States was buying up their assets on the cheap.[15]

But even if the United States, the country with the deepest and most liquid financial markets, could take advantage of the dollar's singular position by selling low-yielding debt securities abroad while accumulating high-yielding foreign direct investments, there was no guarantee that this situation would remain the case indefinitely. While the United States had a head start in the postwar development of its financial markets, given the strict controls that other countries felt compelled to maintain for many years after World War II, increasingly well-developed bank intermediation provided an alternative to securitized finance. Moreover, financial liberalization and development were ongoing. Catch-up in finance was simply one aspect of the broader catch-up process in the OECD over the quarter century following World War II.

And if accelerating inflation raised the danger of capital losses on American investments, other countries would find it less attractive to obtain maturity-transformation services by investing in liquid bank deposits and treasury securities in the United States and receiving less liquid foreign direct investment in return. At some point, the terms of trade might be sufficiently unattractive that short-term capital inflows would stop and even reverse direction. If long-term flows were slower to reverse, as contemporaries assumed, the result could be a crisis for the United States.

Still, from the present-day perspective, the composition of capital flows is a subsidiary issue. The key point is that under the original Bretton Woods system the direction of net American capital flows was strongly outward. Domestic savings exceeded domestic investment all through the 1960s, albeit by a small margin in 1968 and 1969. The excess savings could be invested abroad in earning assets—in the foreign branch plants of corporations headquartered in the United States, foreign government securities, and a variety of other foreign assets—the interest and dividends on which would represent a credit item on the balance of payments. In the event, these expectations of future foreign earnings did not suffice to reassure the markets. But imagine how much worse things would have been and how much more quickly confidence in the system would have ebbed if in addition there had existed other distortions depressing American savings rates and producing current account deficits.

In retrospect, it is striking for how many years jerry-rigged solutions kept the system afloat. Determining whether this past history should be regarded as promising for efforts to keep the current nonsystem afloat requires examining the motives and tactics of officials and policy makers in more detail. Although the reallocation of monetary gold from American coffers to those of the rest of the world was a fundamentally healthy phenomenon—circa 1947 the United States possessed two-thirds of the world's monetary gold, an unsustainably large amount—by the end of the 1950s its share had fallen to less than 50 percent, and the trend was viewed with alarm. The trend in American gold reserves had seemed to turn for the worse in 1958 in the aftermath of the Suez crisis (see figure 1.2). In 1956, the United States had insisted that France, the United Kingdom, and Israel withdraw from Suez, and Washington threatened to use its political leverage to force their compliance if necessary. This episode led to political problems and economic difficulties, most notably in France in 1957 and 1958. In turn, this may have hardened French opposition to the dollar-based international monetary system.[16] Then the shift of the current account from surplus to deficit in 1959 created worries of more deficits to come. For much of 1960, the international monetary intentions of the

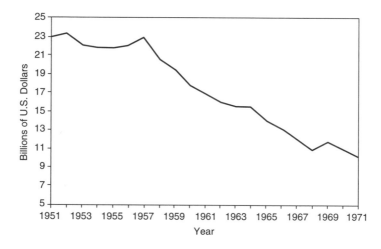

Figure 1.2
U.S. gold reserves, 1951 to 1971
Source: IMF, *International Financial Statistics.*

Democratic presidential candidate, John F. Kennedy, were obscure. His campaign pledge to do whatever was necessary "get this country moving again, to get our economy moving ahead" did not reassure dollar bears.[17] Although Kennedy insisted even before the election that he had no intention of devaluing the dollar, there was a tendency for market participants to reason by analogy with 1933, the last time that a Democrat had taken over from a Republican as president and when one of the new president's first actions had been to raise the dollar price of gold.[18] Thus, prices in the London gold market shot up to $40 shortly before the 1960 American election. Only concerted intervention by European central banks, led by the Bank of England, brought gold prices back down.

Any divergence between the official American and London market prices of gold created a temptation for central banks to buy gold from the United States for $35 an ounce and sell it in London at a higher price. Their capacity to do so was limited only by their liquid dollar reserves. From a collective standpoint, doing so might have been undesirable insofar as it would drain American gold reserves and cast doubt over the country's commitment to convert gold into dollars at a fixed price. But for the individual central bank there was an incentive to engage in such conversions before the gold window slammed shut, as ultimately did happen in 1971, leaving those who had exercised restraint without further options. This created an obvious problem of collective action.

This was the context for the creation of the Gold Pool in 1961. The Gold Pool, discussed at greater length in chapter 2, was an arrangement whereby central banks sought to share the cost of maintaining the London price of gold at $35 an ounce rather than deplete American gold reserves. It encouraged collective action by establishing an understanding of how the costs of these operations would be divided—that is, of what share of the gold that needed to be sold in London to stabilize the market price would be provided by each participating central bank.

But foreign central banks were not prepared to share these costs indefinitely. Even in its heyday, central banks other than the Federal Reserve provided only a third of the gold reserves sold into the pool. Thus, the Gold Pool shifted only some of the pressure of maintaining the $35 gold price in London away from the United States. After the pool collapsed in March 1968, the United States was able to replenish its reserves by attracting capital and purchasing gold from France, where demonstrations spreading from university students to the general public in May created uncertainty about future policy. But this was only a temporary respite. In 1971, Belgium and the Netherlands exchanged dollars for gold, Germany signaled its desire to do likewise, and France indicated that it would demand gold for dollars to make a repayment to the IMF. The last straw came on 13 August, when Britain requested gold. The American gold window was then shut in short order.

Counterfactuals

It is worth asking whether things might have turned out differently. Would more monetary and fiscal restraint by the United States have allowed the Bretton Woods system to continue for a longer period? Could the United States have devalued the dollar against gold and foreign currencies as a way of stemming the secular decline in its current account surplus in the second half of the 1960s?

The answer to the second question has two aspects. First, had the United States raised the price of gold once, it would have almost certainly excited expectations that it was prepared to do so again.[19] An early run on America's gold reserves would have become more likely. A way around this would have been to allow the dollar price of gold to float, as proposed by Allan Meltzer, but this would have meant breaking the gold-dollar link once and for all—something that the United States was unwilling to contemplate until it found itself with no other choice.[20]

Second, there is the question of whether in this period the United States even had the capacity to devalue against the currencies of countries that effectively pegged to the dollar. Foreign central banks and governments could simply follow dollar for dollar, as it were, if the United States raised the dollar price of gold. More than a few countries did just this in 1971, when the United States finally raised the gold price.[21] The episode is not unlike the current situation, in which Asian central banks have been prepared to follow the United States, in their case preventing their currencies from appreciating by buying dollars and accumulating reserves in case the dollar declines against the euro.

On the other hand, would more monetary and fiscal restraint by the United States have permitted this system to stagger on for a significant additional period? In principle, the American government could have raised taxes, and the Federal Reserve could have raised interest rates. By curtailing domestic demand and enhancing the United States' export competitiveness, this would have further strengthened the current account. It is not clear how other countries would have responded. On the one hand, the slower growth of American demand for their exports would have slowed the expansion of their economies, limiting their incentives to respond with parallel policy adjustments. Less inflation in the United States would have enhanced the attractions of tapping the New York market for maturity-transformation services, stimulating capital inflows. For all of these reasons, American gold reserves would have declined less rapidly in this counterfactual scenario. The revaluation of the German mark in 1969, which did so much to signal the impending demise of the dollar standard, presumably would have been delayed.

But it would not have been delayed indefinitely. As the world economy continued growing, other countries would have required additional reserves, and there were few forms in which to obtain them other than liquid claims on the American government—or its gold reserves. Seeing their current accounts weaken and short-term capital outflows to the United States accelerate in response to the American policy initiative, foreign central banks and governments would have had an incentive to tighten monetary policy to offset these effects. The main way in which the day of reckoning would have been delayed in this counterfactual was by slowing the growth of the world economy and thereby the growth in demand for international reserves. The Triffin Dilemma (that for other countries to acquire dollars, the United States had to run deficits, but United States deficits undermined confidence in the dollar) would not have disappeared, in other words, but its consequences would have taken longer to play out.[22]

In practice, central banks probably would have staked out a middle ground between the extremes of doing nothing to sustain economic growth and tightening policy to augment their reserves.[23] When push came to shove, the imperatives of growth dominated the desire to defend the dollar and sustain the operation of the international monetary system. This was nowhere truer than in the United States itself, where policy makers went to considerable lengths to avoid having to adopt restrictive macroeconomic initiatives in support of the exchange rate, insofar as these might slow the rate of growth of the economy and hinder the pursuit of social- and foreign-policy objectives.[24] This explains the extraordinary variety of ad hoc devices to which the United States resorted in an effort to strengthen its balance of payments without having to change monetary and fiscal policies, from soliciting European support for U.S. military commitments abroad to tying foreign aid, tightening limits on the value of duty-free goods that American tourists could bring into the country, imposing the Interest Equalization Tax, and initiating Operation Twist.[25]

Given all this, from the American viewpoint the Bretton Woods system was all too similar to a gold standard of the late nineteenth-century variety, which was ironic given that it was the American delegation that had pushed for gold-standard-like features in the Bretton Woods negotiations. The obligation to convert dollars into gold at $35 an ounce and use of the dollar as international reserves by other countries meant that the

United States could maintain the convertibility of the dollar only through internal deflation, which raised the real value of both monetary gold stocks and official foreign dollar balances and encouraged the production of additional gold in South Africa and elsewhere. In this respect, the dilemma was not unlike that facing the gold standard countries in the 1870s and 1880s. But political constraints on the pursuit of deflation were stronger than a century before. This was true not just in the United States, where there was a demand for both social spending at home and military spending abroad, but also in Europe and Japan, where revaluation would have meant more deflation and less export-led growth. Inflation rather than deflation made it less attractive for foreigners to utilize America's deep and liquid financial markets for maturity transformation services, limiting short-term capital flows toward the United States. Given catch-up and productivity growth abroad, too much inflation in the United States meant too small a current account surplus to finance the country's other obligations.[26] Dollars thus piled up in the coffers of foreign central banks. In turn, this situation led to efforts to negotiate collective restraints on the individual desire to convert those dollars into an alternative asset that might hold its value better before the bottom fell out of the dollar market. These efforts proved reasonably successful between 1961 and 1968, but when they collapsed, it took barely three years for exchange-rate stability under the Bretton Woods system to break down completely.

How the World Has Changed

One way in which the image of a new Bretton Woods system misleads, I have argued, is that it underestimates how dramatically the world has changed since the 1960s. First, the Asian countries that make up the "new periphery" are a less cohesive group than the European countries that dominated the periphery forty years ago. By the 1960s, Europeans had already begun constructing the web of bargains that constitutes the European Union (EU) (formerly the European Economic Community or EEC). In addition, they consulted regularly with one another and with the United States in the Organization for Economic Cooperation and Development (OECD).[27] Indeed, the immediate impetus for transforming the Organization for European Economic Cooperation (OEEC) into the OECD was to provide a mechanism for collective action on the U.S. gold problem.[28] From October 1963 to June 1964, central bank and finance ministry deputies met monthly in Paris under the aegis of the Group of Ten to discuss the operation of the international monetary system. The outcome of their discussions was an agreement to establish a monitoring technology to detect shirking on the commitment to collective action, in the form of a "multilateral surveillance" system obliging all members of the G-10 to provide the Bank for International Settlements (BIS) with data on the means used to finance their payment surpluses and deficits.[29] Group of Ten finance ministers and central bank governors, and their deputies, continued

meeting together thereafter to discuss collective management of the international monetary system. Central
bankers continued to meet monthly at the BIS, and their
regular interaction facilitated negotiation of their gold-
pooling arrangement. Western European countries and
the United States also worked together in the International Monetary Fund, where they were the dominant
voices and where they could thus agree, eventually, to
responses like the creation of Special Drawing Rights.
Thus, governments and central banks had a variety of
mechanisms for acting on the recognition that they had a
collective interest in supporting the dollar, insofar as its
depreciation would undermine their export competitiveness and slow their economic growth. As a result of their
discussions in Basel, it was not even necessary for the
countries that participated in the Gold Pool to draft a
document formally laying out the members' obligations.
Toniolo observes how by November 1961 "the BIS network had engendered sufficient communality of purpose
and mutual trust for the scheme to be agreed there and
then, without a formal written agreement."[30]

In contrast, integration is less advanced in contemporary Asia. Regional free-trade initiatives continue to
stumble. The Association of Southeast Asian Nations
(ASEAN) countries' insistence on exempting sensitive
sectors is impressive even compared to European countries' insistence on protecting their agricultural trade.
There is little agreement on whether to proceed region-
ally (China's preference) or through bilateral agreements

(Japan's alternative). This is just one illustration of the broader inability of the two big Asian countries to work together, in part reflecting their very different stages of economic development (unlike France and Germany in the 1960s) and therefore their different policy priorities. Also symptomatic of the obstacles to regional cooperation is the weakly institutionalized nature of Asian integration. While there exist a variety of groupings (ASEAN, ASEAN+3, EMEAP, and APEC, among others), few are backed by formal institutions (not even a permanent secretariat and certainly not a parliament, commission, and court of justice, as in Europe).[31] The peer pressure, firm surveillance, and political sanctions that encouraged cooperation in Europe in the 1960s still barely exist in Asia today. For all these reasons, mechanisms for containing free-rider problems are less well developed there. Collective action may have sustained the Bretton Woods constellation of exchange rates for thirteen years from the elimination of current account restrictions at the end of 1958 to the closing of the gold window in 1971, but these differences in the institutional setting yield a rather more pessimistic forecast of how many more years the current system will endure.

Second, there now exist more serious rivals to the dominant reserve currency than in the 1960s. Then, the temptation for central banks to diversify out of dollars to avoid capital losses on their reserve holdings was limited by alternatives that were hardly more attractive. The second most important reserve currency, the British pound sterling, was issued by Europe's "sick man." The events of 1967 made clear that shifting out of dollars into sterling was not a way of avoiding capital losses. The French franc was hardly a more attractive reserve asset, a fact driven home in 1969 when the franc was devalued. Japanese financial markets were not sufficiently open to make it attractive to hold yen-denominated assets. While the 1960s was when the Euro-markets and Roosa bonds gained prominence, central banks were reluctant to dabble in private securities or to encourage the development of the euro markets, which were seen as undermining their monetary control. What alternatives did this leave the Bundesbank's reserve managers? Swiss francs? Switzerland was hardly large enough to solve the problem. So long as Germany had no alternative to dollars, the likelihood that all European countries would collectively scramble out of the currency was correspondingly less.

The difference today is the euro. The large, liquid market in euro-denominated government securities provides an attractive alternative to holding United States treasury bonds for the central banks of emerging markets. Together with other pressures enumerated here that suggest the need for the dollar to decline against foreign currencies, including the euro, this alternative becomes even more attractive.

In addition, the one reasonably successful effort at Asian financial cooperation to date is its central banks' and governments' attempt to foster the development of regional bond markets by creating an Asian Bond Fund and pursuing an Asian Bond Markets Initiative.[32] The first $1 billion of reserves devoted to the Asian Bond Fund was invested in the dollar-denominated bonds of Asian governments, but the Asian Bond Fund 2 entails the investment of reserves in local-currency bonds.[33] For the time being, the Asian Bond Fund may still be small in scale, but it creates at least some scope for reallocating reserve portfolios toward assets denominated in regional currencies—scope that is likely to increase over time. As such, it opens up an avenue for reserve reallocation that did not exist in Europe in the 1960s.

Third, there is the fact that in the 1960s the fears of foreign central banks and governments for the stability of their dollar reserves was tempered by the existence of large—and, through the first half of the decade, growing—American current-account surpluses. Because the United States was saving more than it was investing at home, it was investing abroad on net. Its accumulation of foreign assets, which critics like de Gaulle found so objectionable, implied that the global balance of payments would strengthen as the returns on these investments started rolling in. This should have provided at least some reassurance to nervous foreigners. Now, in contrast, the current account is in deficit. While there is dispute over the causes of this increase, majority opinion assigns at least part of the blame to low American savings rates. This means that there is no accumulation of net long-term foreign investments to reassure nervous foreigners (even in the absence of exchange-rate changes) that the United States' balance of payments will naturally strengthen over time.

Fourth, the removal of capital controls makes it harder to bottle up the private-sector portfolio adjustments that must be offset by central banks that are seeking to maintain the prevailing constellation of exchange rates. Asian countries know that they have a collective interest in maintaining their dollar reserves, since selling these will only further weaken the dollar, thus undermining their collective competitive position. Time will tell whether Asian governments and central banks will be able to act on this collective self-interest.[34] Even so, maintaining dollar reserves is not something that motivates private investors, each of whom is interested in maximizing individual returns. A large number of individual and institutional investors, both American and foreign, now participate in the United States treasury market. In the 1960s, the United States could use the Interest Equalization Tax, and foreign governments could employ regulations and controls to limit the reallocation of private investment portfolios and short-selling of the dollar. Yet in principle, American citizens still might have found ways "put" their dollar-denominated assets to foreign central banks.[35] In practice, however, this seems to have happened only to a limited extent.[36] Now, in contrast, the international financial climate is less regulated and more open, and transactions are easier to undertake. If private investors are quicker to act in anticipation of future changes in asset prices, the pressure on central banks and governments will be correspondingly greater.

That financial markets are more open today suggests that the same dynamics will operate more quickly and powerfully, frustrating efforts to put off the day of reckoning regarding the American dollar's exceptional position in international financial markets. This fact is evident even in China, whose capital account is still far from open—although it is growing more open every day. Massive amounts of private financial capital have been flowing into China in response to the recognition that the undervaluation of the renminbi will not be sustainable indefinitely. In response, the Chinese authorities have been forced to sterilize capital inflows. So far, sterilization has not been costly for the People's Bank of China, since the interest rate on domestic debt is even lower than the interest it earns on United States treasury and agency securities. But this convenient situation will not persist indefinitely. It is suggestive of future difficulties that there are already reports of commercial banks growing increasingly reluctant to buy the bills that China's central bank issues in its efforts to sterilize the impact of financial inflows on the money supply.[37] These difficulties will deepen as the state banks are further commercialized and, ultimately, privatized, limiting further the scope for using direct pressure to guide their investment decisions.

Fifth, the domestic financial-market structures in which the consequences of current policies are unfolding are very different than what existed four decades ago. Financial deregulation limits the scope for funneling forced saving into capital formation in the traded-goods sector, which was the strategy of many countries in the 1960s. Keeping exchange rates low in the periphery means keeping interest rates low. Intervening by purchasing dollars means pumping additional domestic credit into the economy, given the limited effectiveness of sterilization. In Japan during the 1960s, much of that additional credit was devoted to capacity building in the traded-goods sector because it was channeled that way by the Postal Savings System, which was controlled by the government, and by the commercial banks, whose investment options were tightly regulated.[38] The situation in Europe was not dissimilar. It is thus possible to argue that in the 1960s the first set of distortions—undervalued exchange rates, artificially depressed consumption, and forced savings—was welfare improving because it offset another set of distortions—that there would have otherwise been too little investment in a traded-goods sector that was the source of positive productivity and growth externalities.

In the twenty-first century's more diversified and deregulated financial environment, in contrast, low interest rates and abundant credit have a greater tendency to spill over into the nontraded goods sector and the property market in particular. Thus, in the 1990s, which was the first time Asian countries pursued policies of export-led growth supported by systematic undervaluation in a significantly deregulated financial environment, a number of them experienced dramatic property-market booms that heightened the fragility of their financial institutions and markets. (Recall the tales of cranes and half built high-rises dotting the Bangkok skyline on the eve of the 1997 crisis.) Now, less than a decade later, the same policies have again produced frightening real-estate booms, not least in coastal China. Asian policy makers are not oblivious to these dangers. As they come to see that undervaluation is doing less to promote exports and more to heighten financial risks, they will have more compelling reasons to let their exchange rates rise.

Sixth and finally, governments in the periphery are aware of this history. The demise of the Bretton Woods system reminds them of Herb Stein's adage that something that cannot go on forever generally will not. Asian policy makers also are aware, precisely because of the historical experience referred to above, that a policy of export-led growth both exacts costs and provides benefits. They are seeking to build more diversified economies that rely on both domestic demand and exports. South Korea, which has sought to stimulate the growth of consumer credit, is a prominent case in point.[39] China is another case where consumption and not exports is now the most rapidly growing component of aggregate demand.

An Alternative Scenario

The United States has little incentive to precipitate the requisite and inevitable adjustment. To the contrary, it is happy living beyond its means. Rather, exchange-rate adjustments will have to be forced by Asia. Eventually, there will be a recognition that policies of export-led growth have reached the point of diminishing returns. This recognition will build on the observation that the traditional traded-goods sectors are no longer the exclusive locus of productivity- and growth-promoting externalities and that activities like software development, back-office services, and financial intermediation are also sources of positive spillovers. Growth will thus require balanced investment in sectors producing nontraded as well as traded goods. Asian countries will have to invest more in higher education. They will have to invest more in housing and urban amenities to make themselves attractive to knowledge workers.

This adjustment on the part of Asian countries will require allowing their real exchange rates to rise. The only way of accomplishing this without compromising price stability will be to curtail intervention in the foreign exchange market. Once one or more Asian countries acknowledge that export-led growth is encountering diminishing returns and curtail their intervention, the cartel of central banks that had been supporting the dollar and preventing Asian currencies from rising will begin to crack. One can imagine a migration out of dollars and into alternative reserve assets, not unlike developments after 1968. Given the low yields on yen-denominated assets, the euro is the obvious direction for such migration.[40] In addition, the commitment of Asian governments to developing a regional bond market may lead them to allocate a growing share of their reserve portfolios to assets denominated in regional currencies.

Inertia is still the single strongest determinant of the composition of central-bank reserve portfolios. Central banks are buy-and-hold investors; they rarely manage their reserve portfolios actively and have a high tolerance for capital losses. It thus is reasonable to anticipate that Asian central banks will not dump their dollars all at once. But there is good reason to think that the adjustment will accelerate with the passage of time.

This move to greater exchange-rate flexibility will be a good thing for Asia. The further decline in the dollar will be a good thing for the adjustment of global payment imbalances. That decline may force the Federal Reserve to raise rates more sharply, curtailing domestic absorption. The increase in funding costs may even cause some future American presidential administration to do something about the country's long-term fiscal problem. This may not be good news for Europe insofar as public and private portfolio reallocation drives up the value of the euro. While Asian currencies may rise against the dollar, the euro will rise also—and to the extent that currencies are driven in the short run mainly by capital flows, on impact the euro may rise against the dollar even more.

These prognostications are necessarily conjectural. Writing the history of the future is harder than writing the history of the past. My reading of the relevant international monetary history is that, while there may be patterns, those patterns do not repeat themselves mechanically. Indeed, there were significant parallels between the Bretton Woods system and the classical

gold standard system that preceded it. But those two systems evolved differently, and their final stages played
out in different ways. Among other things, the Bretton
Woods system was quicker to collapse.

Similarly, there are extensive parallels between the
Bretton Woods system of the 1960s and the revived Bretton
Woods system of our day. But the fact that the original
Bretton Woods system lasted between one and two
decades, depending on how its birth and death are dated,
does not mean that the revived Bretton Woods system will
last as long. Both this reading of history and an appreciation of extent of the differences between the world economy today and that of the 1960s suggest that the end may
not be so long in coming this time around.

2 The Anatomy of the Gold Pool

The Gold Pool is one of the more neglected aspects of the international financial architecture of the 1960s. It was created in 1961 by Belgium, France, Germany, Italy, the Netherlands, Switzerland, the United Kingdom, and the United States to regulate the London price of gold and to share responsibility for stabilizing the market. As such, it was an important aspect of the institutional infrastructure supporting the system of pegged but adjustable exchange rates in the heyday of Bretton Woods.

Yet the Gold Pool receives only passing mention in the standard international monetary histories of the period. Even Robert Solomon, whose *International Monetary System 1945–1976* is otherwise comprehensive, provides only a few pages relating to the Gold Pool's rise and fall.[1] Subsequent histories pay the arrangement even less heed.[2] One possible explanation for this neglect is that few documents relevant to the operation of the pool were published.[3] Another may be the complex and technical nature of the arrangement.

The experience of the Gold Pool, however, is critical for understanding the history of the Bretton Woods system. If this exceptional arrangement was in fact indispensable to the operation of Bretton Woods, then we have yet one more reason to doubt that this system of pegged but adjustable exchange rates organized around gold and the American dollar was stable and sustainable. If the regime's operation hinged on the readiness of official participants not to avail themselves of an essential prerogative on which the regime was ostensibly based—namely, the freedom to convert financial claims on the United States into monetary gold— then we have yet another reason to rethink how we describe the operation of the system currently in place.

As noted in chapter 1, this history also may also shed light on the willingness and ability of countries pegging to the dollar today to resist the temptation of diversifying their reserves for fear of driving up their exchange rates, slowing their export growth, and incurring capital losses on their residual dollar balances. While supporting the dollar may be in the collective interest of America's developing-country trading partners, this does not necessarily mean that it is in their individual interest. Notwithstanding its stake in maintaining the system, each partner country still has an incentive to shift out of dollars to avoid capital losses on its dollar reserves. This will be especially tempting if it can do so without precipitating similar action on the part of other countries—if it can avoid driving the dollar down against other currencies. But if other central banks respond in kind, the dollar exchange rate and the stability of the system may be placed at risk. This is not unlike the situation in the 1960s, when European countries perceived it as in their collective interest to support the dollar and the Bretton Woods system by resisting the temptation to convert dollar-denominated reserves into U.S. gold but where it was in their individual interest to convert their dollars before the price of gold was allowed to rise and the United States shut the gold window.

Dilemmas of collective action can play out in different ways, especially when they occur under different circumstances. The fact that the Gold Pool collapsed in the 1960s does not guarantee the early collapse of the Asian cartel of central banks that currently supports the American dollar. Still, the frequency with which parallels are drawn between the Bretton Woods system and our current constellation of exchange rates and balances of payments suggests that the Gold Pool episode is a useful starting point for thinking about future prospects.

Background of the Problem

A central tenet of the modern international finance literature is that threats to stability are the greatest in periods of transition. Anticipating an impending change in regime, investors have an incentive to act in advance of events. In the international monetary sphere, this means that they have an incentive to sell currencies whose value will be lower in the new regime and to buy those whose value will be higher. In doing so, they intensify the pressure on those seeking to maintain the old constellation of relationships. Their incentive to make profits—or, in the case of central banks, simply to avoid losses—moves up the day of reckoning.[4]

One way of understanding the fragility of the Bretton Woods system is to regard it as a transitional regime. Bretton Woods was a compromise between the gold standard of the late nineteenth and early twentieth centuries, in which each country pegged the domestic price of gold and left gold imports and exports unrestricted, and the post-1971 fiat-money system in which the dollar and other currencies stood in their own right, backed only by the resources of the issuing country and by investors' confidence in the determination and ability of its government to maintain the purchasing power of the monetary unit. Under Bretton Woods, the American dollar was pegged to gold at $35 an ounce, as it had been since 1934. The United States stood ready to convert dollars into gold on demand for official foreign holders but no longer for private investors, domestic or foreign. Other countries, in contrast, could peg either to gold or the dollar. Which they chose was a largely matter of indifference so long as the American commitment to gold convertibility at $35 an ounce was credible. Foreign countries also could adjust their pegs, in either direction, in the event of fundamental disequilibrium.

Thus the Bretton Woods system was a transitional arrangement in that the American dollar was still anchored in gold-standard fashion, while other currencies could move against the greenback, either discretely or in exceptional cases (like the Canadian dollar) continuously, not unlike their position in the post-1971 fiat-money system.[5] Extending to countries other than the United States the prerogative of pegging to the dollar was seen, not unreasonably, as a first step in the direction of demonetizing gold. Allowing the values of other currencies to adjust more freely was seen as a second step in loosening the link between money and gold. Inevitably, these provisions pointed to the question of whether in the future gold would have a monetary role.

From the start, then, market participants had an incentive to speculate that gold might lose its anchor role and that once this happened its price would be allowed to rise. They faced a one-way bet, there being essentially zero probability that the dollar price of gold would fall. Almost immediately following the negotiation of the International Monetary Fund's (IMF) Articles of Agreement, the written constitution of the Bretton Woods system, authors like Robert Triffin conjectured that gold might be on its way out and began warning of the intrinsic instability of the international financial system.[6]

The fundamental factor underlying this one-way bet was the inelasticity of gold supplies. An expanding world economy required an expanding stock of international reserves to be used for smoothing balances of payments and insulating economies from shocks to the international accounts. With the world economy and global trade growing rapidly, the incremental demand for reserves was strong. And in a period when other countries that had suffered relatively severe wartime damage were catching up with the American economy, the demand for reserves grew most quickly outside the United States.

But since governments regulated domestic financial transactions and controlled international capital flows, there were only two attractive forms in which to accumulate reserves. One was gold, for which there existed a market in London and whose value was guaranteed by the American government. The other was dollars, which were backed by the world's largest and most powerful economy, an economy that not incidentally also possessed the world's most liquid financial markets. Other countries lacked liquid markets in financial claims, and the convertibility of their currencies tended to be limited or uncertain. In addition, the continental European countries actively discouraged the holding of their currencies as reserves for fear that their markets would be disturbed and their monetary policies complicated by the large-scale operations of foreign central banks.

Additions to the supply of monetary gold were essentially determined by the capacity of the gold-mining industry, which meant South Africa, Russia, and subsidiary producers like Canada and Australia. As countries directed their monetary policies toward other objectives and inflation accelerated, raising the prices of other commodities relative to gold, allocating resources to gold mining became

even less attractive.[7] Limited additions to the world's stock
of monetary gold did take place (see figure 2.1). But aside
from this modest increase in gold reserves, if the world as
a whole sought additional foreign reserves, it could accumulate these only in the form of dollars.[8] As a consequence,
the stock of dollars held outside the United States in the
form of liquid balances had a tendency to grow relative to
the stock of monetary gold and relative to the stock of monetary gold held by the American government in particular.

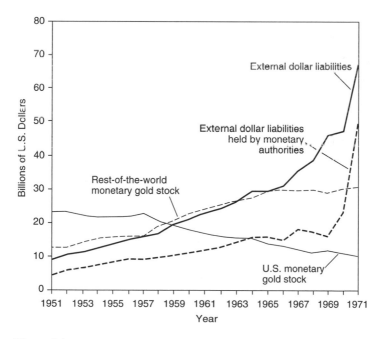

Figure 2.1
Monetary gold and dollar holdings, the United States and the rest of
the world, 1951 to 1971
Sources: IMF, *International Financial Statistics*; U.S. Congress, (1982, vol. 1).

Inevitably, this excited questions about whether the United States could continue to stabilize the relative price of the two assets.

The main factor initially supporting the Bretton Woods system was the disproportionate share of global gold reserves held by the United States. Between the mid-1930s and mid-1940s, the American share roughly doubled, from 35 to 70 percent, the country having taken gold in compensation for its contribution to the war effort. Once World War II was over, some redistribution of monetary gold was logical and desirable. Holding gold rather than just foreign exchange reserves was a traditional choice. Diversifying reserve portfolios in this way was prudent risk management. Thus, as foreign governments and central banks accumulated dollars, they converted a portion of these at the Federal Reserve, redistributing gold from the United States to the rest of the world.

At first, there were few grounds for alarm about the fall in American gold reserves, given the wide margin by which the country's gold holdings exceeded its official foreign liabilities. There was little immediate reason for worrying that the United States would be unable to maintain its commitment to convert dollars held by the foreign official sector at the prevailing $35 price. But as these ratios began to shift, confidence began to erode in the credibility of the American commitment to dollar convertibility and thus in the structure of the Bretton Woods system. By the end of 1959, the United States' money gold stock had been surpassed in value by for-eign-held external dollar liabilities. By 1965, America's stock of gold reserves had been surpassed by the external dollar liabilities held by foreign monetary authorities (again, see figure 2.1). Foreign investors, both official and private, had growing grounds for questioning the ability of the United States to continue honoring its commitment to convert these liabilities into gold at a fixed price.

In London, the main trading center for gold, the exchange houses long had acted as sales agents for newly mined gold from the Commonwealth countries (notably South Africa, Canada, and Australia). Immediately fol-lowing World War II, the Bank of England permitted only limited gold transactions on behalf of nonresidents. The gold market then remained closed between 1947 and 1954 at the IMF's behest. After it reopened, the main market participants were central banks, although private parties assumed a growing role over time.

The spot price of gold in London was market deter-mined, although the price was influenced by official intervention (see figure 2.2). The official price, meanwhile, was set by the American monetary authorities at $35 an ounce plus a small transactions charge.[9] This created the familiar gold-standard dilemma. If the London market price rose relative to the official price, there would be an incentive for central banks to buy gold from the United States at the lower price in exchange for dollar-denominated assets already in their possession and to sell it on the London market at the higher price.[10] Even if

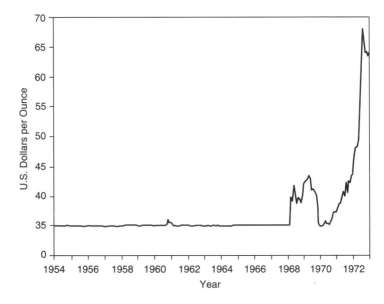

Figure 2.2
London gold prices, 1954 to 1972
Source: IMF, *International Financial Statistics.*

they did not engage in arbitrage, central banks that
needed to sell gold would have an incentive to do so in
the market, while those that needed to buy gold would
have an incentive to purchase it from the United States.
Their separate transactions would indirectly produce the
same result.

The only durable solution was to stabilize the market
price of gold. Given this objective's centrality to what follows, it is worth quoting at length a contemporary explanation of the importance that policy makers attached to
this goal:

The gold pool policy of stabilizing the market price of gold was based on a belief that, if the market price diverged widely from the official price, doubts would arise regarding the viability of the official price. The thought was that some central bankers or finance ministers, seeing a market price of gold at, say $50 per ounce or more, would come to feel that the United States would be unable to hold the official price. Or perhaps some central bankers would buy gold from the United States and sell it at a higher price in the market, thus arbitraging between the two prices. Such doubts, fears, and temptations, if they materialized, would lead central banks to play safe by converting their dollar reserves into gold before others did so and before the United States might be forced either to raise the official price or to embargo official sales of gold. Thus, the market price of gold was regarded as having a monetary significance that justified action by central banks to stabilize it.[11]

Private investors, in contrast to central banks, could not engage in arbitrage, since they could not avail themselves of the U.S. gold window. But they were aware of the incentive for central banks to exchange their dollar assets for American gold reserves if officials saw the market price of gold rise relative to the official $35 price. They understood that if the depletion of American gold stocks persisted, the dollar would ultimately have to be devalued: equivalently, the dollar price of gold would have to be raised. Consequently, they had an incentive to purchase gold, further driving up the market price of the yellow metal, where such transactions were legal. More generally, they had an incentive to shift from dollars toward assets denominated in foreign currencies. The result was capital inflows into the financial markets of strong currency countries, faster expansion of their money supplies, and more inflation.[12]

In principle, central banks could attempt to sterilize the inflow, selling domestic-currency-denominated bonds to mop up its consequences. But the essence of 1960s experience was the suppression of domestic financial markets and hence limited scope for sterilization. The only way of effectively containing imported inflation was thus by revaluing one's currency, something that Germany and the Netherlands did as early as 1961. But revaluation antagonized export interests and jeopardized the prospects for export-led growth. Officials feared that revaluing once would feed expectations that they would revalue again, attracting more capital, fanning inflation, and intensifying the pressure on the dollar.

But simply averring their commitment to the prevailing level of exchange rates did not make the problem go away. Foreign central banks found themselves between a rock and a hard place. If they converted their dollars into gold, they might precipitate the very devaluation that they sought to avoid. But if they waited and other countries proceeded with conversions, they might incur capital losses on their dollar reserves. This was the dilemma that led to the creation of the Gold Pool.

Collective Action

The 1950s had been a relatively placid period for the London gold market, a few flurries like that following the

1956 Suez crisis notwithstanding. Then in October 1960, a number of factors conspired to send the market price of gold up to more than $40 a fine ounce. Market participants speculated that presidential candidate Kennedy's commitment to get the American economy moving again augured more expansionary monetary and fiscal measures that might weaken the balance of payments.[13] They bought gold in London and shifted out of dollars in favor of other currencies. The United States was forced to sell $350 million of gold to the Bank of England in the fourth quarter to stabilize the market. Switzerland purchased gold to offset the inflationary effects of capital flight into its market. Less developed countries, from Argentina to Yugoslavia, purchased American gold to protect themselves against devaluation of the dollar.

In January 1961, President-elect Kennedy reiterated his commitment to maintaining the gold content of the dollar, calming the markets. But political uncertainty over the construction of the Berlin Wall and news of a widening U.S. deficit then precipitated further flight into gold. South Africa and Canada showed a tendency to build up their own gold reserves rather than selling gold into the market, in part reflecting speculative incentives. To prevent the gap between market and official prices from widening further, the United States was again forced to sell gold in London.

By early 1961, the United States' monetary gold stocks had fallen to less than $18 billion. While this amount was still nearly 50 percent of the world total, the prospect of a

further decline was viewed with alarm. Appealing to
Western countries' shared interest in stabilizing currency
values and limiting destabilizing flows of funds, the
United States therefore proposed an informal arrangement
for sharing the cost of this intervention, first to govern-
mental interlocutors and then to central bankers assembled at the Bank for International Settlements (BIS).[14] The
American proposal for a Gold Pool was accepted by seven
European governments in October. Their central banks
agreed to form a sales consortium together with the
Federal Reserve for purposes of stabilizing the gold market. The United States contributed 50 percent of the resources of the pool. Four large European countries—the
United Kingdom, France, Germany and Italy—agreed
to contribute about 10 percent each, while three small
European countries, Belgium, the Netherlands, and
Switzerland, kicked in about 3 percent apiece.[15] The Bank
of England was designated as the operating agent for the
group with the authority to draw on the assembled pool of
gold for intervention purposes.

Between 6 November and 2 December 1961, a successful trial of the arrangement was conducted. Gold prices
then stabilized, allowing intervention to be suspended.
In February 1962, gold prices began to fall, reflecting
Soviet sales. The United States then proposed that the
mechanism should also be used to coordinate purchases
on the London market. Separate purchases by the individual central banks were replaced by buying on the
behalf of the consortium by the Bank of England when-

ever gold was available at or below the United States Treasury's lower dealing margin of $35.08. Purchases were redistributed to the participants according to their quotas in the syndicate. The purchasing consortium reinforced the cohesion of the selling consortium. It provided reassurance that, when replenishing the gold reserves of the participants was possible, this would be done in the same proportions as countries contributed to the sales of the group. Central banks late to the market would not find that other participants had beaten them to the punch. The purchasing syndicate also worked to the advantage of the United States in the sense that prior to the creation of the Gold Pool it had purchased no gold on the London market. Now, when prices were low and central bank purchases were called for, the United States was allocated 50 percent of the gold allotment.

The limitation of the Gold Pool was that there was nothing other than their collective interest in stabilizing the system to prevent central banks from replenishing their gold reserves following sales on their behalf by the Bank of England. They could simply take the dollars thereby acquired and exchange them for gold at the Federal Reserve. American officials had in fact guaranteed this prerogative in 1961 as the price for getting other countries to participate in the arrangement.[16] Hence France, which sought to maintain a high ratio of gold to foreign exchange reserves, automatically reconstituted its gold reserve by purchasing gold from the United States whenever it acquired dollars as a result of Bank of

England operations in London. Thus, while the news that France had left the Gold Pool in June 1967 had a psychological impact, it had few concrete implications for U.S. gold reserves.[17] Switzerland, the Netherlands, and Belgium, three countries that had participated with France in the gold bloc in the 1930s and similarly sought to maintain a high ratio of gold to domestic monetary liabilities, acted in analogous fashion (see figure 2.3). Given the tendency for France, Belgium, the Netherlands, and Switzerland to demand gold as they acquired additional dollars through the operation of the pool, the United States' true share in the pool was more on the order of 70 percent (its own 50 percent plus the collective 20 percent of these four countries).

Keeping that share below 100 percent required moral suasion by the United States to prevent the United Kingdom, Germany, and Italy from similarly demanding gold whenever they acquired additional dollars.[18] The United States possessed leverage over Germany, which still depended on American troops for its defense. Not surprisingly, the German government and the Bundesbank were faithful supporters of the pool and undertook not to convert dollars into gold. The United States also had leverage over the United Kingdom, given the country's weak balance of payments and dependence on the United States Treasury and International Monetary Fund for financial support. Still, the British sometimes wavered in their support of the dollar, since they could ill afford capital losses on their reserves. Italy similarly

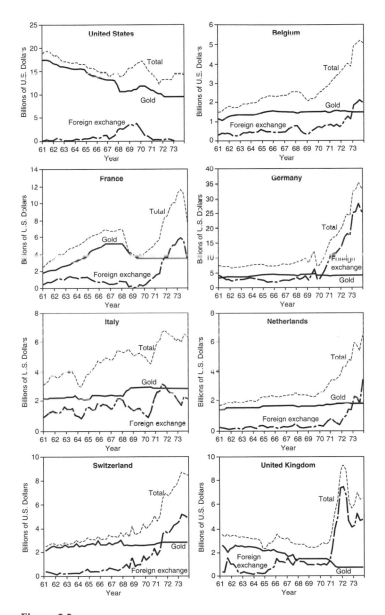

Figure 2.3
Official reserve composition by country: foreign exchange reserves, gold reserves, and total reserves for each member of the Gold Pool
Source: IMF, *International Financial Statistics*.

required financial support from the International
Monetary Fund and the United States Treasury to stem a
run on the lira in 1963 and similarly supported the pooling of gold, but its financial condition strengthened sub-
sequently, at which point it began to express more
reservations about American policies.

The Two Phases of the Gold Pool

The history of the Gold Pool can be divided into two
periods. In its first phase, from 1962 through 1965, the
price of gold was low, as incremental supply, supported
the opening of new South African gold fields in 1961
and 1962, more than matched incremental demand.[19] To
the surprise of its architects, the Gold Pool was a net
buyer of gold to the tune of $1.3 billion (see table 2.1).
With gold reserves, including American gold reserves,
rising continuously, there was less reason to worry
about the stability of the dollar. *Business Week* trum-
peted that the Gold Pool had "[taken all] the fun out of
currency speculation."[20]

This congratulatory evaluation proved premature. From
late 1964, sentiment began to deteriorate. There was the
election of a Labour government in Britain and growing
uncertainty over the future of sterling. Confidence ebbed
further with de Gaulle's 4 February 1965 speech about
the need to restore the gold standard, the escalating of
the war in Vietnam, Chinese gold purchases, and tension
between India and Pakistan.

In the second phase, 1966 to 1968, the price of gold was high, reflecting inflationary pressures and declining confidence in the two reserve currencies on the demand side and declining gold sales by South Africa and the Soviet Union on the supply side. South Africa had experienced balance-of-payments problems and now sought to rebuild its reserves. In addition, the productivity of the mines that opened in the 1950s and 1960s declined with the exhaustion of the most accessible seams. The Soviet Union enjoyed an unusually good grain harvest, reducing its need to export gold for balance-of-payments purposes and similarly allowing it to build reserves. It may also have enjoyed aggravating the monetary problems of the West by holding back production. Global gold production fell in 1967 for the first time since 1953. In the three years 1966 to 1968, the pool was a net seller of gold to the tune of $3.7 billion. These facts help us to understand, even if they do not by themselves explain, the timing of France's decision to leave the Gold Pool in 1967 and the collapse of the pool itself in 1968. Prior to 1966, it had not been necessary for the members to add real resources to the pool. To the contrary, they were in fact able to withdraw resources from the gold market as a result of its operation. Only from 1966 were they required to put their money where their mouths were.

France's reluctance to continue participating was grounded in its leaders' opposition to the asymmetric aspects of the Bretton Woods regime, in which the dollar was pegged to gold but other currencies were pegged to the dollar. The French were critical of a regime in which

Table 2.1
Gold Pool transactions (all figures in $ millions)

Country	Percent	1961–65	1966	1967	Jan. 1968	Feb. 1968	March 1968	Total 1961–March 1968	Total 1966–March 1968
United States	50.000*	+$663.0	–$130.0	–$1,122.7	–$81.8	–$56.3	–$765.0	–$1,492.8	–$2,155.8
Germany	11.111	+207.6	–28.9	–211.6	–15.3	–10.6	–143.4	–202.2	–409.8
France	9.259*	+116.2	–24.1	–5.5	—	—	—	+86.6	–29.6
United Kingdom	9.259	+136.7	–24.1	–176.3	–12.8	–8.8	–119.5	–204.8	–341.5
Italy	9.259	+43.6	–24.1	–176.3	–12.8	–8.8	–119.5	–297.9	–341.5
Switzerland	3.704	+54.6	–9.6	–70.5	–5.1	–3.5	–47.8	–81.9	–136.5
Belgium	3.704	+48.5	–9.6	–70.5	–5.1	–3.5	–47.8	–88.0	–136.5
Netherlands	3.704	+33.6	–9.6	–70.5	–5.1	–3.5	–47.8	–102.9	–136.5
Total	100.000	+1302.4	–260.0	–1,904.0	–138.0	–95.0	–1,291.0	–2385.6	–3688.0

Settlements for 1966: –260.0   Pool gain 1961–1965 +1,345.4

Pool balance Dec. 31, 1965: +42   Pool loss 1966–1967 –2,206.0

Pool balance Dec. 31, 1966: –0–   Net loss 1961–1967 –860.6

Net change in balance	−42.0	
Net pool loss 1966	−302.0	
Pool loss Jan.–June 1967	−101.9	
Pool loss July–Dec. 1967	−1,802.1	
Total loss 1966–1967	−2,206.0	
Pool loss Jan.– March 14, 1968	−1,524.0	
Total loss 1966– Mar. 14, 1968	−3,730.0	
Pool loss Jan. 1968		−138.0
Pool loss Feb. 1968		−95.0
Pool loss Mar. 1968		−1,291.0
Pool pos. Mar. 14, 1968		−3,688.0

*Subsequent to a pool deficit of $320 million, French participation ceased, and the U.S. share became 59.259 percent.

Note: Subtotals may not sum to totals due to rounding and other adjustments.

Source: U.S. National Archives (Treasury Papers).

the dollar, and to a lesser extent sterling, were used to supplement the gold reserves of other countries. As a result, they argued, the reserve currency country enjoyed a looser balance-of-payments constraint. It received a break on the required rate of return on its financial liabilities. This made it easier for the United States to engage in foreign policy initiatives, complicating de Gaulle's efforts to pursue an independent French foreign policy in concert with his European Community partners.

In the French view, raising the price of gold was necessary to reestablish the metallic foundation of the world monetary system. Only then would the value of monetary gold suffice to meet central banks' demand for reserves. Consistent with this preference, France disproportionately held its reserves in gold and thus stood to reap significant capital gains from a rise in its price.

Pressure on the Gold Pool mounted in the first part of 1967. In March, Treasury Secretary Henry Fowler warned that the United States might have to take "unilateral action" to address the ongoing gold drain. In April, the United States quietly notified other countries that if conversions of gold into dollars by foreign central banks continued, it might be forced to alter its policy of making gold freely available to official purchasers. In June, the Six-Day War precipitated a scramble into gold by private investors, forcing the pool to feed the market with $60 million in two days.[21] Then, hopes that the Rio meetings of the International Monetary Fund and World Bank might lead to the early issuance of a synthetic reserve asset, what ultimately became Special Drawing Rights, which would sate the demand for reserves and reduce the official demand for gold, were disappointed. The devaluation of sterling in November then further undermined confidence in the remaining reserve currency, the dollar.

Finally on 21 November, three days after the British devaluation, the fact that France had withdrawn from the pool, something that had taken place five months earlier but been kept secret, was leaked to the markets. The article in *Le Monde* revealing this fact was widely thought to have been written by a French official.[22] Algeria purchased $150 million of gold from the United States, "presumably at French instigation."[23] Rumors appeared in French newspapers to the effect that other countries were preparing to leave the pool. On 23 November, the *Herald Tribune*, also based in Paris, reported that American citizens made up a substantial portion of individuals now buying gold in London.[24]

The members of the Gold Pool responded to this drumbeat of negative news by committing additional resources to their selling syndicate. But as its sales mounted, the European members evinced growing unease about the arrangement. The German government called for a meeting over the weekend of 25 and 26 November to discuss the future of the pool. At that meeting and publicly, American officials reaffirmed their commitment not to raise the dollar price of gold and their willingness to take necessary adjustment measures.[25] In return, the six European members agreed to continue participating in the selling syndicate, although the Bank of Italy, the National Bank of Belgium, and the Netherlands Bank acquiesced only reluctantly.[26] The members of the syndicate enlarged their mutual swap network and secured a commitment from the big private Swiss banks not to accept orders for spot or forward purchases of gold except on margin. But several of the participating countries quickly bought gold from the United States to replace what they had supplied to the pool. Other central banks not participating in the arrangement also purchased gold from the market, ratcheting up the pressure on the countries participating in the pool. In December, identifiable gold purchases in London included those by Malaysia ($7 million), Iraq ($36 million), Kuwait ($52 million), New Zealand ($30 million), Finland ($5 million), China ($33 million), East Germany ($29 million), and other Eastern Europe countries ($5 million). Together their purchases accounted for about one-fifth of all such purchases following the devaluation of the pound.[27] American gold stocks fell by nearly $500 million in the first week of December.

Options for responding to the crisis were discussed at the Basel meeting of central bank governors on 9 and 10 December. These included an American plan for the members of the Gold Pool to create a new reserve asset, a "gold certificate," to replace the gold that the participants in the syndicate were selling in the market. Unfortunately, this scheme did little more than assume a solution to the problem. Given their reluctance to demonetize gold, the willingness of central banks to accept gold certificates in

exchange was limited by the inability of the United States
to credibly guarantee that the certificates would be as
good as gold, any more than it had previously been able to
credibly guarantee that dollars would be as good as gold.[28]

Alternatively, the United States recommended the use
of moral suasion to limit the demand for gold to "normal
commercial requirements." It asked the Bank of England
to approach the five major bullion brokers in London to
provide the names of all buyers on a daily basis. The
Bank of England "reserved the United Kingdom's position" on the advisability of obtaining names for fear that
doing so would diminish the desirability of transacting
in the London market. It worried that such measures
might send buyers to South Africa, where they could purchase gold directly from the producer, or lead to the development of a second gold market in Paris.

By now, the writing was on the wall. Between November 1967 and March 1968, the Gold Pool sold some
$3 billion, roughly 10 percent of the combined gold
reserves of the participating countries. "The Gold Pool is
bad joke," as one Swiss banker put it. "It's all one way.
We've never seen such waves of buying."[29] In the week
ending 1 March, the pool's sales into the market spiked to
$126 million (see table 2.2). But this was nothing com-
pared to the next week, when sales rose to triple that level.
On 13 March, rumors circulated that Italy had defected
from the pool. The following day, the Bank of England
sold $400 million of gold on behalf of the syndicate,
in what were widely described as panic conditions. The

Table 2.2
London Gold Pool: Monthly and weekly transactions, 1968 (all figures in millions of U.S. dollars)

	Net purchase of gold from (+) or sales to (−) the London market	Distribution to members (+) or settlement by collection from members (−)	Cumulative position on account of all pool operations (end of period)		
			Total	Refinanced with FRB	Held in EEA (+) Issued from EEA (−)
Period:					
Jan.	−$138	−$324	−$138	—	−$138
Feb.	−95	−138	−95	—	−95
Mar. to 14th	−1,291	−866	−520	—	−520
Week ending:					
5 Jan.	−3	—	−3	—	−3
12 Jan.	−3	—	−6	—	−6
19 Jan.	−89	—	−95	—	−95
26 Jan.	−41	—	−136	—	−136
2 Feb.	—	−138	−14	—	−14
9 Feb.	−19	—	−33	—	−33

16 Feb.	-10	—	-43	—	-43
23 Feb.	-25	—	-68	—	-68
1 March	-126	-95	-99	—	-99
8 March	-400	—	-499	—	-499
14 March	-792	-771[b]	-520	—	-520[c]

Source: Public Record Office (PRO T267/21).

Notes:

a. Refunded to contributors in February 1962 from surplus arising out of Bank of England operations in the market.

b. Interim settlements by FRB on 12 March ($125 million), 13 March ($100 million), 14 March ($200 million), and 18 March ($350 million), totaling $775 million. Of this, $4 million covers the balance beyond the agreed limit.

c. The UK share is $120 million; other European countries' share is $406 million (to be settled). These sums are to be repaid to FRB.

trading volume of transactions on the gold coin market in Paris reportedly rose to 15 tons, thirty times what had been considered a heavy day. By this time, United States gold reserves had fallen to $11 billion, $10.5 billion of which was required as cover for the note issue.[30]

Overwhelmed by this "gold rush," the British authorities ordered the London gold market closed and declared a bank holiday. The United States suspended the statute requiring gold to be held as backing for the Federal Reserve's note issue. Also on 14 March, U.S. authorities conveyed to their European partners their intention of creating a two-tier gold market in which the market price was allowed to vary but the official price was still pegged at $35 an ounce. A presidential aircraft was dispatched to Europe to collect the governors of the central banks participating in the Gold Pool to secure their agreement.

Meeting in the board room of the Federal Reserve Building on the morning of Saturday, 17 March, the officials representing the other members of the pool were less than pleased. They saw the proposal for a two-tier gold market as indicating the United States' inability to solve the underlying problem and as a first step toward dollar devaluation, which it in fact was. They were unhappy that the United States had announced the new arrangement as a fait accompli. But the scheme at least promised to relieve them of the need to intervene further, and the American proposal was adopted. To provide time for conditions to normalize, the London gold market was kept closed for eleven business days, through Monday, 1 April. The Gold Pool was no more.

Explaining the Collapse of the Pool

The Gold Pool was based on the collective interest of the participating countries in maintaining the dollar peg to gold that anchored the international monetary system. As the Bank for International Settlements put it in 1963, their agreement "was based on the considerations that, as their currencies were convertible through the dollar into gold, wider fluctuations might have implications on the soundness of the value of the currencies of all members of the group and that, therefore, the burden of intervention should be shared by all of them."[31] But while it may have been in the collective interest of the participating countries to limit the conversion of dollars into gold at the Federal Reserve, it was in their individual interest to liquidate as many of those dollars as possible before the United States closed the gold window or raised the official price. Holding together the Gold Pool posed the same problem as holding together any cartel: it was difficult to restrain the temptation for individual participants to cheat on their agreement. And, for a number of reasons, holding the Gold Pool together was even more problematic than holding together a run-of-the-mill cartel.

First, participants in the arrangement did not share a common perception of the problem that their agreement was designed to solve. They did not have a common evaluation of the costs and benefits of their cartel. For the United States, the $35 dollar price of gold that the pool was designed to support was the linchpin of the international

monetary and financial system. Allowing it to give way
would place the entire Bretton Woods system at risk. If the
dollar was devalued against gold, a disorderly round of
competitive devaluations might follow, eroding support
for the multilateral system as in the 1930s. Alternatively,
if the United States was forced to defend its gold reserve
by adopting contractionary policies to strengthen its balance of payments, the world economy might experience
a deflation not unlike that of 1929 to 1931. Starved of
reserves and seeing their balances of payments deteriorate, other countries would slap controls on imports, jeopardizing the Kennedy Round of General Agreement on
Tariffs and Trade (GATT) negotiations and the prospects
for continued export-led growth. In this view, collectively
supporting American gold reserves was in the interest not
just of the United States but of the world.

France's diagnosis, embraced to some extent by
Belgium, the Netherlands, and Switzerland, was different. These countries saw the use of dollars as international reserves as promoting inflation. Because of the
dollar's asymmetric role and the practice by other countries of pegging to the greenback, the United States effectively determined not just its own inflation rate but also
that of the world as a whole.[32] And because American
monetary expansion spilled over to other countries, the
United States had inadequate incentive to internalize the
inflationary consequences of its expansionary monetary
policies. Restoring stability thus required the United
States to rein in its rate of monetary growth, something

that it would do only if forced to strengthen its balance of payments. The French in particular saw purchasing gold from the Federal Reserve as encouraging these necessary adjustments.[33]

Previous studies of international cooperation have emphasized the importance of a common conceptual framework as a precondition for collective action.[34] Lacking a shared diagnosis of the problem, policy makers from different countries are unlikely to be able to sustain a cooperative response. The Gold Pool of the 1960s is a clear instance of this phenomenon. Related to this is the fact that the Gold Pool was seen as facilitating other American policies that were perceived unfavorably by other syndicate members. Those others, first and foremost France, objected that support for the dollar enabled the United States to run more expansionary fiscal policies than would have been possible otherwise. Absent their support, the United States would have been forced to raise taxes and reduce government spending to further strengthen its trade and current-account balances. The pool made it easier for the United States to pursue unilateral foreign policy initiatives, such as its embargo against Cuba and escalation in Vietnam, stances that sat uneasily with European observers.

A second weakness of the Gold Pool was the absence of an enforcement mechanism. The eight-country syndicate lacked mechanisms to sanction members who failed to play by the rules. For France and, to a lesser extent, Belgium, the Netherlands, and Switzerland, the problem was the United States' failure to rein in the continuing flow of dollars that put upward pressure on the price of gold. France demanded more contractionary American policies as a quid pro quo for its membership in the buying syndicate, but it could do nothing to force their adoption other than to threaten to discontinue its participation.[35] Nor could the United States use sanctions to compel foreign support. Faced with the prospect of France's withdrawal, American officials discussed the possibility imposing an embargo on French exports, the imposition of controls on transactions with residents of France in American dollars, and an action in the International Monetary Fund looking toward a formal declaration of the French franc as a scarce currency.[36] Following France's withdrawal, there was also discussion of the possibility of demanding immediate repayment of France's still outstanding World War I debts to the United States.[37] All of these measures were seen, not unreasonably, as having more costs than benefits.

A third weakness was that the cartel was not all-encompassing. There was a "competitive fringe" of small countries in a position to free ride on its operation. Nothing other than moral suasion by countries contributing to the pool prevented developing countries and Middle East oil producers from converting dollars into gold. With the American stock of monetary gold in decline, the costs to Gold Pool members from the existence of this fringe mounted as the period progressed.

A fourth weakness was that the Gold Pool was hard to reconcile with other institutional arrangements. Foreign support for American gold reserves and an agreement on the part of European central banks not to convert dollars into gold were not exactly consistent with the International Monetary Fund's Articles of Agreement. They were hard to reconcile with the official image of Bretton Woods as a decentralized, market-based, symmetric monetary arrangement. Hence the participating countries provided little information about their agreement.

A fifth weakness was that the Gold Pool was not transparent. The participating central banks provided little current information about their reserve operations. The result was uncertainty about whether and when the Gold Pool would intervene and recurrent rumors of its dissolution. The absence of a credible public commitment meant that official intervention did less to stabilize private expectations and market behavior than would have been the case otherwise. As *The Economist* put it in an otherwise laudatory assessment, circa 1962, "The efficacy of the Pool might indeed have been still more spectacular if its activity had not been kept secret."[38]

The most fundamental flaw was that the cartel arrangement was dynamically unstable. As countries grew and their trade expanded, so did their demand for international reserves. The more dollars they accumulated and the longer they resisted the temptation to convert them, the higher the ratio of dollars to gold rose, and the larger the eventual increase in the dollar price of gold that would be needed to restore portfolio equilibrium. As the gap between the current and expected future price of gold widened with the passage of time, it became increasingly tempting to defect from the pool.[39]

Lessons

The idea that Asian countries seeking to prevent their currencies from rising against the dollar face a collective-action problem was discussed in chapter 1. Collective action can be hard to sustain under the best of circumstances. But this chapter's reading of the history of the Gold Pool suggests a number of additional reasons why it may be difficult to hold together the cartel of Asian central banks.

First, today's cartel, just like the Gold Pool, is less than all-inclusive. In the same way that there existed a range of third-world countries and Middle East oil producers actively engaged in converting dollars into gold, today there is a fringe of non-Asian countries, from Russia to Venezuela, with the incentive and ability to diversify their reserves. The more dollars that they liquidate, the more dollars that must be absorbed by Asian central banks seeking to prevent the dollar's fall. In the presence of such a fringe, cartel-like behavior is more costly, and the probability of sustaining it is lower.

Second, the fact that central banks are less than transparent about their reserve-management policies complicates the task of holding together the cartel. Only a small number of central banks, twenty-one at the time of writing, publish information on the currency composition of their international reserves through the International Monetary Fund's Special Data Dissemination Standard. Typically, they do so only annually. At last report, the only Asian economies on this list were the Philippines and Hong Kong. The less information is shared by governments and central banks and the longer the lag with which they share it, the more likely they are to think that they can diversify out of dollars without being noticed and precipitating a rush for the exits. Edwin M. Truman proposes that more countries should be encouraged to provide information on reserve composition with at most a quarterly lag.[40] This may happen one day perhaps, but the opacity of current reserve-management practices does not bode well for the cohesiveness of the cartel.

Third, there is the absence of an enforcement mechanism—of credible sanctions to be applied to Asian countries that curtail their accumulation of dollars and diversify their reserves.

Finally, there is the fact that the country whose currency is the recipient of this support, the United States, is not a member of the relevant regional arrangements. When the Gold Pool first came under strain, the United States sought to reassure its partners that their financial commitments would be limited by promising to implement balance-of-payment measures of its own. The Organization for Economic Cooperation and Development and Bank for International Settlements offered convenient venues for discussions of the reciprocal policy adjustments to which the United States would be party. Today's Executives'

Meeting of East-Asian Pacific Central Banks and Association of Southeast Asian Nations are less well suited for this purpose, since the United States does not belong. Global institutions like the International Monetary Fund, for their part, are too large and unwieldy.

Balance requires acknowledging the existence of factors working in favor of the status quo. One is the absence of an Asian Charles de Gaulle—a political leader set on divesting the dollar of its status as the world's leading reserve currency and seeking to alter the structure of the international system. De Gaulle was willing to subject the world economy to serious dislocations if doing so was necessary to achieve his ends. Someday Asia may acquire its de Gaulle. One can imagine an intensification of geopolitical rivalry between China and the United States that, in the future, prompts Chinese leaders to withdraw their support for the dollar and seek to transform the international system. For the time being, however, Chinese leaders clearly have no desire to kill the golden goose.

The most important factor supporting the status quo is the existence in Asia of a shared development model. The prevailing regional development paradigm still centers on export-led growth. Given the priority attached to exports, Asian governments and central banks are concerned not to precipitate a sudden fall in the currency of the country constituting their principal external market. To the extent that global imbalances must be reduced through the adjustment of exchange rates, they prefer to see this happen gradually in a gradual manner that does not disrupt the growth of foreign sales. This perception of a common development model provides a basis for discussing what shared policies are best suited for facilitating this gradual adjustment.

Slowly but surely, however, Asian countries are moving away from the traditional model of export-led growth supported by an undervalued exchange rate. They are doing so at different rates. It follows that some Asian countries are more ready than others to see a fall in the dollar. And as countries continue to develop divergent views of the priority that should be attached to a stable, competitively valued exchange rate, collective action to support the dollar will become more difficult to sustain.

That the Gold Pool collapsed after six years and barely two years after sustained sales of gold commenced does not guarantee that Asian support for the dollar will collapse within a similar time frame. Important differences between the 1960s and the current international monetary situation cannot be denied. Still, the Gold Pool reminds us that governments seeking to prevent a fall in the currency issued by the country that is their principal export market face a problem of collective action. And its history reminds us that when institutional support is weak, when information is imperfect, when a fringe of nonparticipating countries exists, and when views of the nature of a desirable outcome begin to diverge, sustaining cooperation can be problematic.

3

How to Exit a
Currency Peg: Japan
and the End of the
Bretton Woods
System

For the better part of a decade, ending in the summer of
2005, China pegged its currency to the American dollar at
what amounted to a fixed rate of exchange. For China,
this was a dynamic period of rapid export-led growth
accompanied by large and growing external surpluses.
For the United States, it was a period of large and growing external deficits. This imbalance was the context for a
contentious debate over the advisability of the peg for
China itself and its implications for the world economy.
For China, the question was whether revaluing against
the dollar and embracing greater exchange-rate flexibility would kill the golden goose of export-led growth or
whether such adjustments would simply allow its monetary authorities to steer the economy more effectively. For
the rest of the world, the question was whether a Chinese
revaluation and a move to greater flexibility were needed
to redress the problem of global imbalances. When in
July 2005 the Chinese authorities announced a 2 percent

With Mariko Hatase.

revaluation and their intention of moving gradually to greater flexibility, the questions became whether this modest revaluation was enough, whether the Chinese authorities really were prepared to countenance a significant increase in currency flexibility, and what the effects on economic growth would be.

There are few precedents for these questions. In particular, it is hard to think of many large, export-oriented, fast-growing economies in the early stages of catch-up that have exited voluntarily from a peg.

However, Japan at the end of the Bretton Woods period offers one precedent for this type of action. After two decades of pegging at 360 yen to the dollar, Japan decoupled from the dollar on 28 August 1971, repegging on 18 December at 308 yen in conjunction with the Smithsonian Agreement (the international agreement to realign currencies and widen bands but otherwise maintain the façade of the existing international monetary system). The new peg lasted fourteen months, after which greater flexibility was introduced.

This chapter uses this historical precedent to shed light on the controversy over China's currency policy. It argues that there are extensive parallels between the two cases, not least the reluctance of policy makers to contemplate a significant revaluation, given more than a decade of successful export-led growth. The parallels extend even to the specifics of the adjustment when it ultimately came—a one-time step revaluation followed after a period by a gradual shift to freer floating.

At the same time, the analogy must be developed carefully. Japan then was more advanced than China is now. Japan's per capita income was higher, and its economy was closer to the technological frontier as defined by the United States. While government involvement in the economy was extensive, that involvement was not as pervasive as in China. Japan also had more sophisticated financial markets and a better-developed monetary transmission mechanism. Still, and notwithstanding these differences, Japan's experience from the 1950s through the 1970s can provide useful insight into China's monetary options today.

Background

Japan in the 1950s and 1960s, like China in the 1980s and 1990s, grew at rates far in excess of those witnessed anytime in its previous history. GNP growth in Japan between 1955 and 1971 averaged 9.3 percent per annum. This was a dramatic acceleration from 1913 to 1950, when growth had averaged 2.0 percent, and from 1885 to 1913, when it had proceeded at a 2.6 percent yearly pace.[1] China's economy has expanded at nearly 10 percent per annum since economic reforms commenced in 1978, which is a similar revolution in growth performance.

In Japan after World War II, as in China today, growth was fueled by exports, facilitated by the transfer of advanced technology, sustained by investment, and supported by elastic supplies of cheap labor. Exports grew at an annual average rate of 17 percent between 1955 and 1971, more than half again as fast as output.[2] Exports quadrupled in volume between 1959 and 1969 and increased by a further one-third in the next two years, impressive performance even by contemporary Chinese standards. Associated with these trends were a doubling of Japan's share of the rest of the world's imports in the course of the 1960s and especially rapid growth in the share of American merchandise imports accounted for by Japanese suppliers (see table 3.1). Japan's surplus with the United States was more than $1 billion in 1970, reflecting the buoyant American market for the country's exports of consumer goods in conjunction with Japan's need to finance imports of energy and raw materials from other suppliers. Strong surpluses allowed Japan to more than double its foreign reserves in the final part of the 1960s.

By the end of the 1960s, Japanese gross national savings rates had risen to 40 percent and the investment-to-GNP ratio had reached 35 percent, levels comparable to China's today (see table 3.2). Employment in agriculture declined by 3 percent per annum in the second half of the 1950s and the first half of the 1960s, offset by the rapid growth of employment in the modern sector, led by manufacturing, facilitating industries, construction, and services. More than 70 percent of Japan's full-time farm households were underemployed after World War II.[3] Elastic labor supplies could thus be made available to industry without driving down agricultural output.[4] Contemporaries referred to a dual wage structure in

Table 3.1
Exports and the current account

	Japan			China		
	Export Growth (annual average, percentage)	Share of U.S. Imports (percentage)	Current Account (billions of U.S. dollars)	Export growth (annual average, percentage)	Share of U.S. Imports (percentage)	Current account (billions of U.S. dollars)
1950s	12.4%	3.9%	$0.1		0.2%	
1960s	16.6	10.8	0.3		0.0	
1970s	14.6	13.3	3.1	13.5%	0.2	
1980s	5.3	18.5	42.0	25.0	1.4	–$1.8
1990s	2.3	15.6	99.4	23.4	6.4	12.5
2000s	3.5	10.7	114.0	22.4	10.4	24.4

Sources: IMF, *Balance of Payments Statistics;* IMF, *Direction of Trade Statistics;* IMF *International Financial Statistics;* Bank of Japan, *Balance of Payments Monthly;* National Bureau of Statistics of China, *China Statistical Yearbook 2001;* Yamazawa and Yamamoto (1978).

Notes: Export growth is based on national currency-denominated figures. Share of U.S. imports is calculated using U.S. dollar-denominated figures. Share of U.S. imports since 2000 is calculated using data for 2000 to 2003. China's current account figure for the 1980s is the average for 1982 to 1989. That since 2000 is the average for 2000 to 2002. Japan's current account for the 2000s includes data through 2004.

Table 3.2
Savings and investment rates (percentage)

	Japan		China	
	Savings Rate	Investment Rate	Savings Rate	Investment Rate
1950	29.9%	16.2%		
1960	34.1	30.2		
1970	40.5	35.1		
1982			34.0%	32.1%
1990			38.0	35.2
2000			38.7	36.2
1950s: 1st half	27.5	20.1		
2nd half	29.0	24.4		
1960s: 1st half	35.8	32.4		
2nd half	37.0	32.4		
1980s: 1st half			34.5	33.2
2nd half			35.9	37.5
1990s: 1st half			39.9	38.5
2nd half			40.7	38.5

Sources: Ohkawa, Takamatsu, and Yamamoto (1974, tables 1A, 6A); National Bureau of Statistics of China (2001, tables 3–11); IMF, *International Financial Statistics.*

Notes: Japan's rates are relative to GNP; China's are relative to GDP. China's savings are the sum of gross capital formation and net current account. Figures for the first half of the 1980s cover 1982 to 1984.

which the wages of employees of enterprises in the modern sector were at least twice the levels of those in the agricultural sector—indicative of a strong incentive for labor reallocation.[5] In all these respects, the parallels with contemporary China are clear.

But there are also important differences. At the beginning of its high-growth period, Japan was a relatively advanced industrial economy, reflecting the development of a modern textile industry in the nineteenth century and then steel and shipbuilding in the first half of the twentieth century. China, in contrast, had a dearth of modern industry when embarking on reform in 1978. Japanese per capita GDP in 1950 expressed in 1990 international Geary-Khamis dollars was $1,926, whereas Chinese per capita GDP in 1978 was $979. Five years later, the comparable figures were $2,772 and $1,265.[6]

The Japanese system of technology transfer was also different. Whereas China today relies on foreign direct investment (FDI) for technology transfer, Japan relied on licensing and reverse engineering. The Japanese government limited inward FDI for three decades after 1950. Mark Mason and other researchers argue that restricting market access for foreign multinationals facilitated the country's efforts to license foreign technologies.[7] They conclude that the relatively advanced state of the Japanese economy, together with the lower tacit component of advanced technology compared to today, ensured the effectiveness of this approach to technology transfer.

The structure of labor markets was different as well. In Japan during the 1950s, labor was free to move from the countryside to the cities; the freedom to select one's occupation and place of residence were individual liberties guaranteed since the early Meiji period. In contrast, the Chinese authorities still attempt to regulate the movement of the rural population to the cities in order to avoid threats to the public order, using a system of official work permits or visas. The effectiveness of these measures is difficult to evaluate since illegal internal migration is rife. So too are the implications for the China-Japan comparison. On the one hand, China today has even larger reserves of underemployed rural labor anxious to find work in the high-wage modern sector. On the other hand, labor's freedom to move is less.[8]

In addition, the banking and financial system was stronger in Japan. Banks were not burdened by the overhang of nonperforming loans plaguing the big-four banks in China. Their lending decisions were guided by commercial motives, although subject to window guidance (quantitative limits on the growth of lending by individual banks, described in more detail below). The lending charges of Japanese banks could be adjusted freely (even if published lending rates were relatively stable, the banks still adjusted the compulsory deposits required of their customers). In China, banks have less freedom to adjust lending rates, and in any case such rates matter less for lenders and borrowers with soft budget constraints.

Monetary control in the two countries exhibits both similarities and differences. Japan had a sounder banking and financial system than China has now. At the same time, given the extent of controls and the Bank of Japan's (BOJ) reliance on directed credit, there is a sense in which the mechanisms of monetary control were not all that dissimilar. In the 1950s, the BOJ used the discount rate, discount-rate surcharges for excess borrowing, and window guidance to influence the growth of money and credit.[9] It used changes in reserve requirements, which altered the banks' capacity to lend, starting in 1959. From the mid-1950s, it also sold short-term government securities. The BOJ purchased and sold bonds, especially after the government resumed issuing these in 1966. It purchased private bills (prime bills or promissory notes issued by banks with prime bills attached as collateral, which were introduced in 1972).

Open market operations of the normal sort did not really exist, since there was little in the way of a liquid bond market. Japan's central bank rationed discounts and loans against bills. It gave window guidance to the large city banks in the 1950s and then to the long-term credit banks, large regional banks, and trust banks in the 1960s. It used a variety of informal tools for controlling corporate bond issuance.[10] When selling government bonds in the late 1960s, the BOJ informally allocated these to banks in specific amounts. This reliance on moral suasion resembles current practice in China, where the authorities similarly attempt to influence bank lending and credit conditions by instructing the banks to limit and adjust their lending to accommodate the objectives of monetary policy.

To be sure, the extent of these practices differed across markets. The call market tended to be subject to controls, though the intensity of restrictions changed over time. "The experts including the authorities considered that the level of call rates was abnormally high" in the early stage of the high-growth era and, thus, moral suasion by the BOJ or self-imposed restrictions by financial institutions on call rates were believed to be necessary.[11] However, the coverage of these restrictions was limited, and there were loopholes allowing effective rates to fluctuate to some extent. Thus, "call loan rates worked as indicators for the condition of financial market as a whole though the function was imperfect."[12] Yields on government-guaranteed bonds, bank debentures, and corporate bonds in secondary markets could fluctuate relatively freely, while those in primary markets were kept at artificially low levels.

Finally, compared to China today, government involvement in the Japanese economy was less extensive. To be sure, volumes have been written about the industrial policies of the Ministry of Trade and Industry and the credit-allocation policies of the Ministry of Finance. The Japanese government sought to channel resources into industrial development, establishing the Reconstruction Finance Bank, which was eventually taken over by the Japan Development Bank (JDB), and the Export Bank of Japan, which was renamed the Export-Import Bank of Japan (Ex-Im Bank). These public financial institutions influenced economic development through the Fiscal Investment and Loan Program (FILP). The FILP was overseen by the Ministry of Finance, which collected public deposits through the Postal Savings System (and the resources of the public pension system) and passed them on to the JDB, the ExIm Bank, and other public financial institutions such as the Housing Loan Corporation.

The commercial banks, in contrast, retained basic autonomy over their loans and investments within ceilings set by window guidance.[13] There was no counterpart in 1950s and 1960s Japan of the nonperforming-loan problem in contemporary China.[14] This suggests that the extension of credit for noneconomic reasons was less than in China today. While it is hard to put precise figures on the share of policy loans in the portfolios of Chinese state banks, it is fair to say that the banking system, which is heavily dominated by state banks, has devoted more of its resources to development lending, not always with positive results for bank balance sheets and for the development of the Chinese economy.

Currency Policy

For nearly a quarter of a century after World War II, Japanese currency policy was predicated on an exchange rate pegged to the dollar and stringent capital controls. The yen was pegged at 360 on 25 April 1949 in conjunction with the Dodge Line (the macroeconomic stabilization program implemented under the guidance of the U.S. occupation authorities).[15] It remained there until the collapse of the Bretton Woods system in 1971.

Exchange-rate stability has been portrayed as integral to the Japanese economy's growth and to the growth of its exports in particular.[16] To be sure, in strong upswings, the demand for imports grew more rapidly than the supply of exports, and export supply was partially crowded out by domestic absorption. It was not possible to finance the resulting current-account movements with foreign reserves, since prior to the mid-1960s the government followed a strategy of limiting reserve accumulation to be able to plow resources into fixed investment. This meant that Japan's central bank had to tighten to restrain the growth of demand, limit the deterioration of the external accounts, and defend the currency peg. This constraint on the rate of growth was referred to as the "balance-of-payments ceiling."[17] Fortunately, this constraint bound only at high rates of growth, at least after the beginning of the postwar period.

This observation has led observers to ask whether the yen was significantly undervalued during this era. The consensus appears to be that the currency was overvalued at the start of the postwar period but that overvaluation gave way to undervaluation in the course of the high-growth years.[18] Until the currency was pegged in April 1949, there had been debate between Japanese officials and the Economic and Scientific Section of the Supreme Commander for the Allied Powers (SCAP) over its appropriate level. SCAP proposed a rate of 330 to the dollar, but Japanese officials preferred a lower rate in part because they anticipated that sterling and other currencies might soon be devalued against the dollar.[19] The Bank of Japan observes that, at the eventual rate of 360 to the dollar, "the exchange rate was considerably overvalued given the effective price level considering black market prices. It was a challenge to adapt the Japanese economy to the newly set exchange rate."[20] As Ryutaro Komiya puts it, "The exchange rate of 360 yen per dollar set in 1949 was significantly overvalued compared with the equilibrium rate at which the external accounts are balanced without restrictions on imports and without export enhancement policies."[21] Yutaka Kosai agrees with the proviso that overvaluation emerged only after sterling was devalued and inflation accelerated with the outbreak of the Korean War.[22] These observations suggest at least some qualification of the conventional wisdom that an undervalued exchange rate was central to Japan's postwar growth from the start.

Initially, tight foreign-exchange controls were needed to support the currency. But with the recovery of the economy following the imposition of the Dodge Line and the rapid growth of productivity in the traded-goods sector in particular, what had once been seen as an overvaluation was increasingly seen as an undervaluation.[23] Government-led rationalization of the metals, machinery, and chemicals sectors led to reduced production costs in industries in which Japan already had some presence. In addition, at the end of the 1950s and increasingly in the 1960s, Japan's export competitiveness was enhanced by technological progress and structural change leading to the emergence of new export products that had not been produced before in significant quantities or even at all, such as plastics, business machines, and automobiles.[24]

Already at the end of the 1950s, Miyohei Shinohara used comparisons with the 1930s to argue in favor of undervaluation.[25] While there is some debate over precisely when this undervaluation emerged, by the late

1960s there was considerable evidence in favor of the hypothesis. By this time, Japan had learned to produce many of the capital goods needed for its industrial expansion rather than importing them from abroad. After 1965, the current account moved into surplus, and then from 1968 foreign reserves rose strongly. The balance-of-payments ceiling of which observers had warned no longer seemed to constrain growth even in strong expansions.[26]

To analyze these questions further, nominal and real effective exchange rates for the 1950s and 1960s were constructed.[27] These series are trade-weighted averages of bilateral nominal rates for seventeen leading trading partners accounting for 40 to 50 percent of total Japanese exports. Figure 3.1 for the nominal exchange rate shows

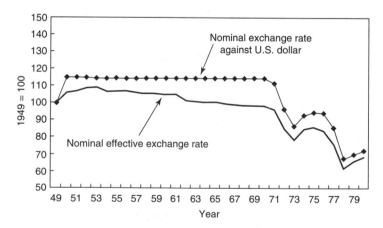

Figure 3.1
Nominal effective exchange rate (1949 = 100)
Sources: See the data appendix to chapter 3.

that focusing exclusively on the yen-dollar exchange rate, as is typically done in discussions of the post–World War II years, understates currency variability. It also shows a tendency for the nominal effective rate to appreciate over the high-growth period as a result of devaluations against the dollar and thus the yen by other countries.[28]

Figure 3.2 plots wholesale prices in Japan relative to wholesale prices in other countries converted into yen (the real exchange rate). We see how the real rate rose around the time of the Korean War, consistent with the emphasis of Yutaka Kosai.[29] It then fell by 3 percent from the mid-1950s through the late 1960s, although the bilateral

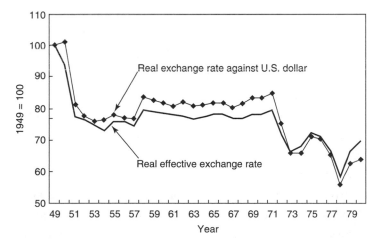

Figure 3.2
Real effective exchange rate (1949 = 100)
Sources: See the data appendix to chapter 3.

real rate against the U.S. dollar fell by about twice this amount.[30] This is consistent with the hypothesis of emerging undervaluation, although the change in the real effective rate is small. Note also that while the real bilateral rate against the United States continued to depreciate in the second half of the 1960s, the real effective rate did not. Figure 3.2 thus suggests that back-of-the-envelope calculations based on American and Japanese inflation rates, together with the constant bilateral exchange rate, tend to exaggerate these trends.

It can be argued that relative wholesale prices adjusted for exchange-rate changes understate the change in competitiveness, since wholesale prices are dominated by homogeneous goods whose cost tends to be driven to equality by arbitrage. A better comparison for Japan would be the unit prices of exports relative to other industrial countries, since most Japanese exports were differentiated manufactures and the developed countries were Japan's main competitors in markets for these products. Figure 3.3 confirms that export prices rose less rapidly than wholesale prices over the high-growth period, especially in the early 1950s.

Figure 3.4 shows the unit value of exports since 1951 relative to the advanced economies.[31] It indicates a substantial one-time improvement in Japan's international competitiveness in the first half of the 1950s, as emphasized by Miyohei Shinohara.[32] There is then a further improvement as the high-growth period proceeds.

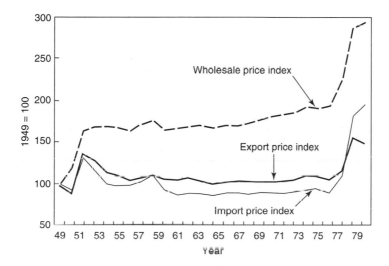

Figure 3.3
Prices (1949 = 100)
Source: Ohkawa et al. (1967).

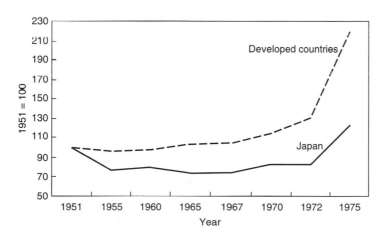

Figure 3.4
Unit price of exports (1951 = 100)
Source: Nakamura (1993, p. 214, table 61).

Export prices fell by 7 percent between 1960 and 1962, led by declines at twice this rate in three industries that had been the targets of government-led rationalization and modernization investment: metals, machinery, and chemicals. After this time, the unit value of Japanese exports held steady or rose slightly in periods when raw material prices were rising, but competitiveness continued to improve as a result of inflationary developments abroad and relatively rapid Japanese productivity growth and technical change. Overall, Japanese export prices fell by 29 percent relative to those of its industrial-country competitors between 1951 and 1967. All this suggests growing undervaluation.

Exiting the Peg

Whether overvalued or undervalued, Japan's government took the peg at 360 yen to the dollar as an "immutable condition."[33] When Germany's economy minister Ludwig Erhard visited Japan in 1958 and argued that the government should allow the currency to appreciate as part of a strategy of reducing government intervention in the economy, his remarks elicited a strong negative reaction. The day following Erhard's remarks on the revaluation of the yen, Japanese Finance Minister Eisaku Sato commented at the press conference, "Though Economy Minister Erhard said that one of the causes for extremely cheap prices of Japanese goods is the level of exchange rate, the current exchange rate of 360 yen per dollar is not undervalued. If

Japan revalued its exchange rate, Japanese trade industries could not cope."[34]

Until Germany floated the mark in May 1971, the issue of yen realignment was the subject of little systematic planning.[35] Even then, Finance Minister Mizuta continued to insist that "the best policy choice is to achieve economic stabilization under the fixed exchange-rate regime."[36] Those few economists and officials who did consider the possibility of revaluation tended to dismiss it as damaging to exports, investment, and confidence.[37] Fears that changing the exchange rate would have negative implications for employment growth and security in the manufacturing sector led some observers to warn that tampering with the exchange rate could even provoke political unrest.[38]

Of course, those advocating maintenance of the dollar peg had to offer alternatives for countering the chronic current account surplus, which caused tension with foreigners, and for how to handle the inflationary pressures associated with capital inflows.[39] The dominant recommendation was to relax exchange controls and trade barriers to encourage imports. Kamekichi Takahashi stressed the need for import liberalization.[40] The government in fact pursued this option by selectively removing foreign exchange controls and import quotas and relaxing regulations limiting outward FDI.[41] Others, like Osamu Shimomura, plumped instead for fiscal stimulus to encourage imports and rebalance the current account.[42] Still others worried that this option would intensify inflationary pressure. What is striking in retrospect is that there was virtually no discussion of the possibility of a revaluation to offset what had become a substantial external surplus, coupled with fiscal stimulus to sustain growth as demand rotated away from net exports.

Symptomatic of the deeply ingrained nature of inherited policy, Japan continued to peg the yen to the dollar by intervening in the foreign-exchange market for two weeks after President Nixon closed the gold window. The combined reserves of the central bank and the Ministry of Finance rose by nearly 50 percent between 16 August, the day following Nixon's decision, and 27 August. After 27 August, the BOJ stopped purchasing dollars at the old price of 360 yen. The yen was allowed to appreciate, although the BOJ still intervened to slow its movement, accumulating more reserves. When the yen reached 308 to the dollar, a 16.9 percent bilateral appreciation, it was repegged. The discount rate was cut and intervention was reinitiated as needed to prevent the nominal rate from appreciating further. The BOJ cut its discount rate by 50 basis points in December 1971 and again in June 1972.

Expectations were that revaluation would slow the growth of exports. In addition, it was argued that abandoning the dollar parity that had been the anchor for policy since the late 1940s had negative effects on investor confidence.[43] Companies would be led to postpone investment and run down their inventories. In response, a supplementary budget was passed for April 1971 to March 1972, and a more expansionary stance was adopted for fiscal year 1972 with expenditures on general account up by 22 percent and expenditure on public investment and lending through the FILP up by 32 percent over the previous year.

These measures, combined with continued strong growth of the world economy, were key to Japan's smooth adjustment to the new exchange rate, as is shown below. After a pause (the economy bottomed out in December 1971 according to the business-cycle dates of the Economic Planning Agency), real GNP grew by more than 10 percent on an annualized basis in the first quarter of 1972.

When the Smithsonian Agreement collapsed in early 1973, the yen was again allowed to float upward, this time to 265. Consistent with the advice tendered to China today, Japan's float was heavily managed: the exchange rate was limited to a narrow range between 264 and 266 yen to the dollar through September 1973.[44]

Capital Controls and the Forward Market

Throughout this period, exchange and capital controls remained in place. Restrictions on convertibility for purposes of transactions on the current account were maintained well into the 1960s. Foreign-currency transactions relating to imports required a license from Ministry of International Trade and Industry (MITI), while all foreign-currency transactions for other purposes, such as transactions related to inward foreign direct investment

(FDI), required one from the Ministry of Finance. Capital-account transactions were essentially suppressed. Up through 1963, the current account balance and changes in foreign reserves moved in lockstep, reflecting these pervasive controls on capital account.

The first step in liberalization was the establishment of yen accounts for foreign residents of Japan in 1960. The authorities then eliminated restrictions on current-account transactions in April 1964, accepting Article VIII of the Articles of Agreement of the International Monetary Fund. Inward investment was liberalized in 1968, but even then it was not entirely free: significant restrictions on inward FDI remained into the 1970s.

The 1949 Foreign Exchange and Foreign Trade Control Law, which remained in effect until 1980, prohibited individuals from holding foreign exchange except with the permission of the authorities. There were also restrictions on the ability of Japanese financial institutions to maintain open positions in foreign exchange and on the ability of foreign financial institutions to take positions in domestically issued yen-denominated securities.[45] From 1968, restrictions on open positions were supplemented and then largely superseded by swap limits (yen conversion quotas under which the authorities set a ceiling for net short spot positions in foreign currencies plus the amount of outstanding free yen liabilities to nonresidents).[46] This had the effect of limiting covered interest arbitrage, causing the forward rate to move more freely and making speculation more costly.[47]

Some of these restrictions were tightened in the early 1970s, when the yen was unpegged, with the goal of limiting capital inflows. In 1972, controls were tightened on advances against exports, additional reserve requirements were imposed on increases in nonresident yen deposits, and limits were placed on nonresident purchases of Japanese securities.[48] Then in 1973, when Japan's current account swung into deficit, first with the strong expansion of the economy and then the OPEC shock, controls on capital inflows were abolished while those on outflows were reinforced. When the yen strengthened in 1977, controls on the foreign-currency deposits of residents were abolished, measures prohibiting residents from acquiring short-term foreign securities were eliminated, and a 50 percent reserve requirement on increases in the yen deposits of nonresidents was instituted.[49] Indicative of the extent of these capital controls, covered interest parity (the interest differential between the United States and Japan adjusted for the difference between spot and forward exchange rates) held closely after December 1980, the moment of deregulation, but not before.[50]

The development of the forward foreign-exchange market depended on the relaxation of exchange controls and but also on the incentive to invest in forward cover.[51] The collapse of the Bretton Woods system triggered an increase in transactions on the forward market. To be sure, these transactions only began rising after the short-run disruption had passed, since the markets temporarily stopped functioning with the yen's floating in August

1971.[52] Exchange controls were then tightened, resulting
in a lack of opportunities for arbitrage and the further
drying up of forward-market transactions. The market
then reopened in late October.[53] But from there the growth
of the forward market was explosive (see figure 3.5).
Evidently, the development of a reasonably deep and liquid forward market depended not just on the stringency
of controls but also on the incentive to insure against
exchange-rate fluctuations, which developed only after
the transition to a more flexible rate.

Turning to the question of China's monetary policy
today, some skeptics of the feasibility of a more flexible
renminbi argue that full currency convertibility, including
on capital account, is a necessary prerequisite for greater

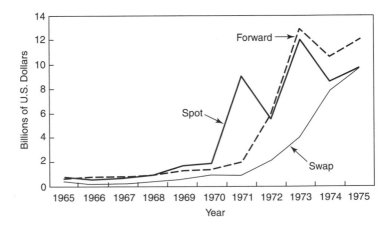

Figure 3.5
Foreign-exchange transaction volume, 1965 to 1975
Source: *Nihon Keizai Shinbun* (Nikkei Newspaper).
Note: Intraday trading volume is averaged for December of each year.

exchange-rate flexibility in practice. Others suggest that floating requires a deep and liquid forward market and that China should not permit the renminbi to vary more freely and be determined by market conditions until there is significant additional progress in developing the interbank forward market in Shanghai. Japan's experience is not consistent with this view. While controls had been partially relaxed prior to floating the yen, these were still far from eliminated.[54] This history does not suggest that it is necessary to finish liberalizing the capital account and developing the interbank forward market before moving to a more flexible exchange rate. It suggests that corporations can hedge at least some of their exposures despite the maintenance of residual capital controls. It suggests that the development of forward-market liquidity is, at least in part, endogenous to the monetary regime; greater flexibility will help to produce the larger volume of transactions desired by the authorities. And it suggests that banks and firms in China now, like those in Japan after 1973, should be able to tolerate a further increase in exchange-rate volatility so long as the central bank continues to intervene to avoid very sudden movements in the currency's level and sharp spikes in volatility.

Effects of Exiting the Peg

Efforts to identify the impact on Japan of exiting the peg are complicated by other disturbances that hit the economy around this time. By the early 1970s, the

high-growth period following World War II was coming
to an end; after two decades of rapid export- and invest-
ment-led growth, much of the productivity gap between
Japan and the United States had been closed. While the
average annual rate of GDP growth decelerated from 12.1
percent in 1960 to 1969 to 7.5 percent in 1970 to 1973 and
3.8 percent in 1973 to 1985, it would be a mistake
to attribute the entire shift to the change in exchange-rate
regime, since with the end of the catch-up period there
would have been some slowdown in any case. In addition, the world economy grew rapidly for two years following Japan's exit from the peg, which may have
cushioned its economy from any disruptive effects.

As emphasized earlier, the motors of Japanese growth
were exports and investment. One way of isolating the
impact of the shift in the exchange rate on growth is therefore to examine its effect on these two variables. Figure 3.6
juxtaposes capital investment in the manufacturing sector
(as a share of GDP) with the real effective exchange rate.
Investment shot up once the real exchange rate came
down in the wake of the Korean War; it then declined in
the early 1970s coincident with the appreciation of the real
rate. The movement of manufacturing profits (current
profits of the manufacturing sector as a share of GDP),
upward after the early 1950s and then down after 1971, is
consistent with the operation of this mechanism, with
causality running from international competitiveness to
manufacturing profitability and from there to capital formation in the manufacturing sector.

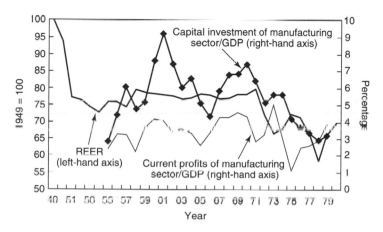

Figure 3.6
Real effective exchange rate (REER) and investment (1949 = 100; percentage)
Sources: Japan Ministry of Finance (1977); Economic and Social Research Institute (n.d.).
Note: For REER, see the data appendix.

This analysis is complicated because other things were happening at the same time, some of which could have been affecting the real exchange rate, profitability, and investment. The technological progress and industrial rationalization in the 1950s emphasized by Shozaburo Fujino and Yutaka Kosai would have affected Japanese economic growth precisely by stimulating profitability and investment in manufacturing.[55] The rapid growth of the world economy in 1971 to 1973 and the policy stimulus applied by the Japanese authorities could have supported investment and profitability in the face of a negative exchange-rate shock.

A more systematic analysis of the connections between the exchange rate and investment is therefore required. A previous study along these lines is by Tsutomu Miyagawa and Joji Tokui,[56] who regress gross investment in manufacturing as a share of the capital stock on the real exchange rate and a vector of controls (a proxy for global demand, the ratio of wages to the cost of capital, and the ratio of intermediate input prices relative to the cost of capital).[57] They confirm that appreciation (depreciation) of the real effective exchange rate had a negative (positive) impact on Japanese investment in the 1980s.[58] This is in line with the findings of other studies, where real appreciation reduces export prices relative to costs, squeezing profitability and discouraging investment.

We extend their analysis back to the 1950s and consider not just the bilateral rate against the dollar but the real effective exchange rate. We estimate an equation of the form:

$$i_t/k_{t-1} = \alpha + \beta\, reer_{t-1} + \gamma w_{t-1}/c_{t-1} + \delta\, d_{t-1}/k_{t-1} \qquad (3.1)$$

where i is real capital investment in manufacturing, k is real capital stock in manufacturing, $reer$ is real effective exchange rate, w is the real wage in manufacturing, c is user cost of capital, and d is world income.

We lag the independent variables, assuming time to build, and enter the wage and cost of capital in ratio form (consistent with a Cobb-Douglas production function). The GDP of major industrial countries d is our proxy for global economic conditions. It is normalized by the capital stock following the specification in Miyagawa and

Tokui.[59] All variables are annual, and the sample period is 1955 to 1973.[60]

A problem with estimating this relationship in levels is that many macroeconomic time series exhibit unit roots. The augmented Dickey-Fuller test confirms that the real exchange rate and the factor price ratio have unit roots. In contrast, the hypothesis of a unit root can be rejected at the 1 percent level for the investment ratio and world income normalized by the capital stock.[61] Estimating this relationship in first differences consequently may introduce a problem of overdifferencing.

We therefore estimated the equation both in levels and differences. Table 3.3 shows the results. When the relationship is estimated in levels, the real effective exchange rate enters significantly, with a positive coefficient, indicating that appreciation had a negative impact on manufacturing investment.[62] The real wage relative to the user cost of capital is significant with a positive sign, indicating that a change in relative factor prices induces capital/labor substitution, other things equal.[63] World income is also significant with a positive sign, confirming that an increase in world income had the expected positive effect on investment. The results using the differenced data, in the second panel, are consistent with these findings.

The effect of the exchange rate on exports during high-growth periods is one of the major issues in the studies described above. In table 3.4 we estimate an export function like that specified by Takafusa Nakamura:[64]

$$ex_t = \alpha + \beta \, reer_t + \gamma d_t \qquad (3.2)$$

Table 3.3
Determinants of investment

Annual Data

Estimated equation: $i_t/k_{t-1} = \alpha + \beta\,reer_{t-1} + \gamma\,w_{t-1}/c_{t-1} + \delta\,d_{t-1}/k_{t-1}$

Figures in parentheses are t-statistics.

Levels

	Real Effective Exchange Rate	Real Wage / User Cost of Capital	World Income	Adjusted R²	DW Statistic
Constant term					
−28.63	6.13	0.61	0.62	0.50	1.14
(−2.20)*	(2.46)*	(1.99)*	(2.35)*		

Differences

	Real Effective Exchange Rate	Real Wage / User Cost of Capital	World Income	Adjusted R²	DW Statistic
Constant Term					
0.05	3.14	0.86	1.22	0.21	1.32
(0.60)	(1.88)*	(2.50)*	(2.04)*		

Source: See the data appendix to chapter 3.
** Denotes 1 percent significance; * denotes 5 percent significance.

Table 3.3 (continued)

Notes: 1. User cost of capital is calculated as follows:

$$r = P_c * (i - \pi + d) / P_w$$

where r is user cost of capital, P_c is price index of capital goods (1952–1960) or of investment goods (1960–1971), P_w is wholesale price index (WPI), i is banks' lending rate (the average rate on bank loans in December of each year), π is percentage change in WPI, and d is the depreciation rate.

2. For details on the construction of the real effective exchange rate, see the data appendix to chapter 3.

3. Capital investment in the first quarter of 1955 is assumed to be the same as the averaged amount of the second to fourth quarters. Capital stock at the end of 1952 is assumed to be the same level as that of the end of March 1953.

4. Real wage is total cash earnings per regular employee in the manufacturing sector deflated by the WPI.

5. World income is aggregated real GDP of eleven countries (see the data appendix to chapter 3).

6. World income is normalized by the capital stock, following Miyagawa and Tokui (1994).

Table 3.4
Determinants of exports

Annual Data

Estimated equation: $ex_t = \alpha + \beta\, reer_t + \gamma d_t$

Figures in parentheses are t-statistics.

Levels

Constant Term	Real Effective Exchange Rate	World Income	Adjusted R^2	DW Statistic
-13.45	0.89	3.05	0.99	1.19
(-9.65)**	(3.12)**	(72.32)**		

Differences

Constant Term	Real Effective Exchange Rate	World Income	Adjusted R^2	DW Statistic
0.04	1.04	2.27	0.35	2.08
(0.85)	(3.13)**	(2.23)*		

Table 3.4 (continued)

Sources: Japan Ministry of Finance, *Financial Statements and Statistics of Corporations* (Hojin Kigyo Tokei), various issues; IMF, *International Financial Statistics*, various issues; *Direction of Trade Statistics*, various issues; Maddison (2001); Mitchell (1998a, 1998b, 1998c); Japan Ministry of Trade and Industry, *Annual Report of the Foreign Trade of Japan* (Nihon Boueki Nenpyo), various issues; Bank of Japan (1986); Bank of Japan (1987), *Hundred-Year Statistics of Wholesale Prices in Japan.*

** Denotes 1 percent significance; *denotes 5 percent significance.

Notes: 1. Exports are deflated by the export price index on a long-term economic statistics (LTES) basis (1953–1959) or a WPI basis (1960–1971).

2. For details regarding the construction of the real effective exchange rate, see the data appendix.

3. World income is the aggregated real GDP of eleven countries (see the data appendix).

where *ex* is real exports, *reer* is real effective exchange rate, *d* is world income, and α, β, and γ are the parameters to be estimated.

The results, again estimated over the period 1955 to 1973 with annual data, are shown in table 3.5.[65] Here estimates using the differenced data are more reliable given that we fail to reject the null hypothesis of a unit root in all series.[66] The real effective exchange rate is significantly positive, confirming that the appreciation negatively affected Japanese exports. Global income is significant with a positive sign, again consistent with previous studies.

Simulating the impact of exiting the peg on Japanese investment and exports requires an estimate of by how much the real exchange rate changed given the post-1970 adjustment in the nominal exchange rate. Since regressing the real exchange rate on the nominal exchange rate would put the nominal rate on both sides of the equation, we instead estimate a pass-through equation, regressing the wholesale price index (WPI) on the nominal effective exchange rate, foreign WPIs, and relevant controls. Since the real exchange rate is the ratio of domestic prices to foreign prices adjusted for the nominal exchange rate, the results can be used to estimate the impact of nominal appreciation on the real exchange rate (and hence on real variables like investment and export volumes).

The long-run relationship is of the form

$$wpi_t^{JP} = \beta_0 e_t + \beta_1 \, wpi_t^{For} + \Omega X + \varepsilon_t \qquad (3.3)$$

Table 3.5
Long-term passthrough (quarterly data)

	(1)	(2)	(3)	(4)
Nominal effective exchange rate (ln)	0.142 (0.030)***	0.142 (0.030)***	0.136 (0.028)***	0.137 (0.029)***
Weighted foreign price level (ln)	0.354 (0.048)***	0.354 (0.048)***	0.555 (0.064)***	0.555 (0.064)***
Oil price (ln)	0.114 (0.013)***	0.114 (0.014)***	0.061 (0.017)***	0.061 (0.017)***
GDP (ln)	0.067 (0.006)***	0.057 (0.006)***	0.160 (0.022)***	0.161 (0.022)***
Quarterly dummies	No	Yes	No	Yes
Trend	No	No	Yes	Yes
Observations	136	136	136	136
R^2	0.99	0.99	0.99	0.99

Sources: IMF, *International Financial Statistics*, various issues; *Direction of Trade Statistics*, various issues; Maddison (2001); Mitchell (1998a, 1998b); Japan Ministry of Trade and Industry, *Annual Report of the Foreign Trade of Japan* (Nihon Boueki Nenpyo), various issues; Bank of Japan, *Hundred-Year Statistics of Wholesale Prices in Japan*; Yamazawa and Yamamoto (1978).

*Significant at 10 percent; ** significant at 5 percent; *** significant at 1 percent.

Note: Standard errors in parentheses.

where wpi^{JP} and wpi^{For} are the logs of the Japanese and weighted average of foreign wholesale price indices, e is the log of the nominal effective exchange rate (yen per unit of foreign currency), and x is a vector of controls (quarterly dummies, a linear time trend, real GDP, and the natural logarithm of the oil price, which figured importantly in Japanese price trends in the 1970s and 1980s).[67]

The equation is estimated using quarterly data for 1957 to 1990. The pass-through coefficient in table 3.5 is in the range of 0.1 to 0.2. Using data for a later period, José Manuel Campa and Linda S. Goldberg obtain a long-run pass-through coefficient for Japan of 0.8, but they consider import prices rather than wholesale prices.[68] Wholesale prices are likely to move less insofar as these include a large component of domestic prices that are less affected by exchange-rate changes. Pass-through coefficients for other large economies such as the United States using relative wholesale prices also generate estimates on the order of 0.2.

A potential problem is that it is not possible to reject the hypothesis of a unit root in the dependent and independent variables (see table 3.6). However, these results will be consistent if the individual series are cointegrated. It is appropriate therefore to test for the presence of unit roots in the residuals. The tests in table 3.7 indicate that the null hypothesis of a unit root can be rejected.

The next step is estimating a short-run relationship that will allow for a more accurate characterization of adjustment dynamics. Using the residual from the preceding

Table 3.6
Unit root tests (generalized Dickey-Fuller test, all variables in logs)

Variable		No Trend	Trend
WPI Japan	Level	0.108	−15.40
	First difference	−3.744***	−4.211***
Nominal effective	Level	0.972	0.568
exchange rate	First difference	5.332***	5.200***
Weighted foreign	Level	0.578	−1.621
price level	First difference	−2.616***	−2.980***
Oil price	Level	0.312	−1.482
	First difference	−5.002***	−4.900***
GDP	Level	0.090	−0.522
	First difference	−1.019	−3.935***

*, **, *** Indicates unit root hypothesis can be rejected at 10 percent, 5 percent, and 1 percent significance levels, respectively.

Note: All tests include a constant and four lags.

Table 3.7
Unit root tests (generalized Dickey-Fuller test)

	No Trend	Trend
Equation 1	−1.653	−3.086**
Equation 2	−1.706	−3.115**
Equation 3	−1.692	−2.875*
Equation 4	−1.741	−2.899*

Sources: Input prices for export sectors are calculated using input price indices for industries whose export dependence in 1974 and 1975 was more than 20 percent: precision instruments, transport equipment, steel, general machinery, and textiles. Input price indices for these sectors are aggregated using their weights in the 1970 input price index. The source is Bank of Japan, *Price Indexes Annual*, various issues.

*, **, *** Indicates unit root hypothesis can be rejected at 10 percent, 5 percent, and 1 percent significance levels, respectively.

Note: All tests include a constant and one lag.

regression, denoted u_t, as the error correction term in an equation designed to capture short-term dynamics,

$$(3.4)$$

Solving this equation for the long-run effect of nominal appreciation on domestic prices (long-run pass-through), we obtain

$$(3.5)$$

Estimates are provided in table 3.8. Now long-run pass-through is even smaller than before. However, the point estimate is noisy due to the inclusion of γ^0 and γ^1 coefficients that are statistically indistinguishable from zero. To correct for this, we recalculated ϕ excluding γ coefficients that were not statistically significant at the 10 percent level. The pass-through coefficient derived in this manner (ϕ') is also reported in table 3.8. Now the results are more stable across specifications, suggesting a long-run pass-through coefficient of 0.25.

A possible concern is that these results may be excessively influenced by the pre-1971 period when the yen was pegged to the dollar. Since the change in the nominal dollar rate was zero in this period, pass-through from the exchange rate to prices will be zero by construction.[69] Two approaches were employed to addressing this problem. First, the sample was restricted to the period after

Table 3.8
Pass-through dynamics

	(1)	(2)	(3)	(4)
Δp_{t-1}	0.633	0.651	0.631	0.649
	(0.092)***	(0.093)***	(0.095)***	(0.096)***
Δp_{t-2}	−0.101	−0.119	−0.122	−0.140
	(0.108)	(0.111)	(0.112)	(0.114)
Δp_{t-3}	0.025	0.036	0.013	0.023
	(0.095)	(0.096)	(0.098)	(0.099)
Δe_t	0.091	0.089	0.087	0.085
	(0.027)***	(0.027)***	(0.027)***	(0.028)***
Δe_{t-1}	−0.007	−0.004	−0.006	−0.003
	(0.031)	(0.031)	(0.032)	(0.032)
Δe_{t-2}	−0.016	−0.022	−0.01	−0.016
	(0.031)	(0.031)	(0.031)	(0.031)
Δe_{t-3}	−0.038	−0.033	−0.031	−0.026
	(0.030)	(0.030)	(0.030)	(0.031)
Δp_t^*	0.283	0.267	0.275	0.259
	(0.098)***	(0.099)***	(0.100)***	(0.101)***
Δp_{t-1}^*	−0.058	−0.032	−0.089	−0.063
	(0.109)	(0.111)	(0.113)	(0.114)
Δp_{t-2}^*	0.219	0.200	0.203	0.184
	(0.108)**	(0.109)*	(0.111)*	(0.112)
Δp_{t-3}^*	−0.101	−0.098	−0.125	−0.121
	(0.092)	(0.093)	(0.094)	(0.096)
Δoil_t	0.030	0.030	0.028	0.027
	(0.009)***	(0.009)***	(0.009)***	(0.009)***
Δoil_{t-1}	−0.021	−0.021	−0.014	−0.015
	(0.009)**	(0.010)**	(0.009)	(0.009)
Δoil_{t-2}	−0.015	−0.013	−0.011	−0.009
	(0.011)	(0.011)	(0.011)	(0.011)
Δoil_{t-3}	0.000	−0.001	0.005	0.004
	(0.010)	(0.010)	(0.010)	(0.010)

Table 3.8 (continued)

	(1)	(2)	(3)	(4)
Δgdp_t	0.003	0.001	0.023	0.021
	(0.059)	(0.059)	(0.064)	(0.065)
Δgdp_{t-1}	0.090	0.094	0.107	0.11
	(0.056)	(0.057)	(0.062)*	(0.062)*
Δgdp_{t-2}	−0.000	−0.008	0.006	−0.002
	(0.059)	(0.059)	(0.063)	(0.063)
Δgdp_{t-3}	0.033	0.036	0.033	0.036
	(0.054)	(0.054)	(0.058)	(0.059)
$\hat{\mu}_{t-1}$	−0.153	−0.154	−0.13	−0.130
	(0.039)***	(0.039)***	(0.039)***	(0.039)***
φ	0.069	0.068	0.085	0.084
	(0.106)	(0.109)	(0.100)	(0.103)
φ'	0.249	0.256	0.237	0.243
	(0.102)**	(0.109)**	(0.101)**	(0.108)**
Quarterly dummies	No	Yes	No	Yes
Trend	No	No	Yes	Yes
Observations	132	132	132	132
R^2	0.75	0.75	0.74	0.74

*Significant at 10 percent; ** significant at 5 percent; *** significant at 1 percent.

Note: Quarterly data, standard errors in parentheses.

the peg was abandoned. The coefficient on the nominal exchange rate turns out to be roughly the same as before, suggesting that any attenuation problem is not serious.[70] Second, a dummy variable was created for the floating period to interact with the nominal exchange-rate terms; this vector was added to the explanatory variables. This result provides a direct test of the hypothesis that pass-through changed with the shift from pegging to floating. The long-run regression now becomes

$$wpi_t^{JP} = \beta_0 e_t + \theta_0 e_t * D^{PEG} + \beta_1 wpi_t^{For} + \Omega X + \quad (3.6)$$

where exchange rate pass-through is now given by $\phi'' = \beta_0 + \theta_0$. The results confirm that pass-through was significantly higher in the floating period.[71] But the additional effect is small; it has little impact on the overall level of long-run pass-through as estimated above.

Recall that the nominal effective exchange rate appreciated by 11.0 percent between 1971Q2 and 1971Q4. Assuming a pass-through coefficient of 1/4, the induced appreciation of the real rate was three-quarters of this, or 8.3 percent. This is close to the actual appreciation of the real effective rate between 1971 and 1972 (see figure 3.2).[72] Between 1971Q1 and 1973Q1, the nominal effective rate rose by 26.2 percent. Three-quarters of this is 19.7 percent. Again, this is close to the actual real appreciation observed in this period. We therefore take a real appreciation of 8.3 percent as the short-run impact and 19.7 percent as the longer run impact of the exit.

We now are in a position to calculate the impact of the change in the nominal effective exchange rate on exports and investment. Taking the coefficients estimated on first-differenced data in tables 3.3 and 3.4, the short-run (1971 to 1972) fall in exports is 8.6 percent. The longer-run (1971 to 1973) fall is 20.4 percent. The impact on investment is larger: its level declines by 11.1 percent between 1971 to 1972 as a result of the 8.3 percent real appreciation. The long-run effect is four times as large.

These results for exports and investment are consistent with one another. Figure 3.7 suggests that Japanese firms responded to the short-run move in the exchange rate by cutting margins: they did not raise prices commensurately, which meant that businesses absorbed the much of the impact.[73] The fact that export prices did not rise as

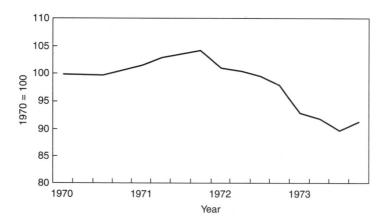

Figure 3.7
Export price index/Input price index of export sectors
Source: See the data appendix to chapter 3.

quickly as consumer and wholesale prices in 1971 and 1972 is consistent with this fact. In turn, the decline in margins had a sharp negative impact on investment, which contributed to the recession that started in 1973. Why then was a sharp slowdown in Japanese exports, investment, and growth not observed in 1972 and 1973? The results suggest that the contractionary impact of appreciation on exports was offset by the rapid growth of world income, which rose by a cumulative 12 percent in these two years. This illustrates the advantages of exiting from a peg while global demand conditions are favorable (which is one of the principal conclusions of the literature on exit strategies).[74] Japan in the 1970s would seem to be a prime case in point.

Japanese investment demand and demand more generally were sustained by expansionary fiscal policies. As noted above, the government quickly submitted a supplementary budget and raised current expenditures for the year immediately following by more than 20 percent. This stimulus sustained domestic demand even while the growth of external demand was being curtailed by real appreciation. Note that these are precisely the kind of domestic policy adjustments recommended for sustaining growth in China at the same time the real exchange rate is allowed to rise.[75]

In addition, the Bank of Japan applied a large dose of monetary stimulus in the effort to limit the yen's appreciation. Real interest rates declined sharply: although the WPI increased by 15 percent in 1973, the nominal bank lending rate rose only 1 percent. These expansionary monetary policies were not without cost. Inflation rose alarmingly as the authorities ramped up money supply growth to prevent the yen from rising further. Consumer-price-index (CPI) inflation rose from 5 percent in 1972 to 12 percent in 1973 and then 23 percent in 1974, when the oil shock hit.[76] At that point, the authorities were forced to apply the brakes, precipitating a major recession. A better course, in retrospect, would have been a tighter monetary policy that allowed the currency to continue appreciating against the dollar, with the impact on aggregate demand cushioned by additional expansionary fiscal policy.

Conclusion

This analysis of Japan's currency experience in the 1970s suggests a number of parallels with China today. Like China now, Japan had enjoyed over a decade of rapid export-led growth based on an exchange rate pegged to the American dollar at competitive levels. Like policy makers in China now, policy makers in Japan then were reluctant to mess with success. They were reluctant to exit the dollar peg despite persistent external surpluses and growing difficulties of steering the domestic economy. Like Chinese officials now, Japanese officials warned that industry could not survive a substantial revaluation. They worried that the absence of deep and liquid currency forward and futures markets limited the ability of banks and firms to hedge foreign exposures, making a floating exchange rate potentially destabilizing. When revaluation finally came, it was not obviously destabilizing. The decline in net exports was offset by buoyant global demand. Investment demand and domestic demand generally were supported by generous fiscal stimulus. The Japanese authorities limited exchange-rate volatility by heavily managing the float, in effect providing the hedging services needed by banks and firms and minimizing the consequences of the limited liquidity of currency forward markets and the retention of capital controls.

This analysis of Japanese currency experience in the 1970s suggests that a rapidly growing, export-oriented economy can successfully navigate the transition to greater exchange-rate flexibility so long as the authorities sensibly manage the resulting float. Allowing the currency to vary enables the authorities to tailor money and credit conditions to domestic needs as the economy moves from a monetary and financial system that relies on administrative guidance to one in which interest rates guide the allocation of credit and financial markets become increasingly open to capital flows. But it is important for the country to manage its exchange rate with domestic conditions in mind and to avoid the kind of large real appreciation that would significantly compromise profitability and investment.

In addition, this analysis of Japanese experience does not suggest that the move to greater exchange-rate flexibility must wait on the elimination of capital controls and the complete development of deep and liquid foreign currency forward and futures markets. To be sure, free flexibility could jeopardize financial stability in the absence of deep and liquid forward markets on which foreign exposures could be hedged. But by managing the float through intervention in the foreign-exchange market, the central bank can in effect provide the hedging services that private markets cannot. Moreover, allowing the exchange rate to fluctuate more widely can create a demand by corporations for these hedging services, in turn encouraging the development of the relevant financial markets. The development of those markets requires only that capital controls be loosened, not that these be eliminated entirely.

Moreover, this analysis suggests that supportive changes in domestic policy, fiscal policy in particular, are important for easing the transition. Japan deployed fiscal policy to offset the contractionary effects of revaluation in the early 1970s. China, where the unmet demand for health care, education, and other social services remains intense, has scope for doing likewise.

A final lesson of Japanese experience in the early 1970s concerns the advantages of exiting while the going is good—while global economic conditions are favorable and external demand is growing strongly. Japan faced favorable global demand conditions in the early 1970s. From the mid-1990s, China has similarly reaped benefits from a rapidly growing world economy. But the favorable environment benefiting the Japanese economy dissolved suddenly, starting in 1973. The danger is that China could find itself with a similar problem in the not-too-distant future.

A substantial revaluation is advocated in some circles as China's contribution to reducing the United States' current account deficit. But if Japan's experience in the 1970s is a guide, then a large step appreciation risks damaging profitability and investment and thus slowing economic growth. A Chinese "contribution" to global rebalancing that has this effect is in no one's interest. A more prudent course of action would be gradual adjustment that does not kill the golden goose of economic growth, complemented by financial restructuring and a significant dollop of fiscal support. It would be better if these constructive policy adjustments in China were accompanied by appropriate monetary and fiscal adjustments in the United States so that this country also contributes to resolving the problem of global imbalances that are largely of its own creation.

Appendix

Nominal Effective Exchange Rates (NEER)

Nominal effective exchange rates (NEER) consist of yen exchange rates against the currencies of seventeen countries: the United States, the United Kingdom, West Germany, Greece, Italy, the Netherlands, Sweden, Switzerland, Canada, Venezuela, Australia, India, Iran, South Korea, Thailand, the Philippines, and South Africa. These are the countries that meet the following criteria: imports from Japan in 1960 exceed 10 billion yen, and both price data and foreign-exchange-rate data series are available from 1949 to 1990. (South Korea is an exception as its wholesale price index is not available in 1950. As figures in 1949 and 1951 are identical, we assume that the WPI in 1950 was unchanged from 1949.) The seventeen bilateral rates are weighted by the value of imports from Japan, updated every five years. Note that the series depicted in figure 3.1 excludes nominal exchange rate against South Korea as its extreme increase (its level in 1970 is 300 times larger than that of 1949) dominated the trends of other currencies.

Real Effective Exchange Rates (REER)

Real effective exchange rates (REER) consist of yen exchange rates against the currencies of the same seventeen countries. Each nominal exchange rate is normalized by the wholesale or producer price indices of Japan and the country in question and weighted as above. For Japan's wholesale price indices, the domestic wholesale price index is used from 1960 while the overall wholesale price index, which includes export and import prices, is used to 1959 due to data constraints. Note that figure 3.2 excludes the real exchange rate against South Korea for the same reason as above. Among the econometric results reported in the text, those that contain the data for the mid-1950s (namely, investment and export equations) exclude South Korea from the weighted average to avoid the effects of the high-inflation episodes at the time.

World Income (D)

We estimate world income by aggregating the GDPs of eleven countries: Australia, Belgium, Canada, France, Germany, Italy, Japan, Sweden, the Netherlands, the United States, and the United Kingdom with import value-based weights in 1955, 1960, 1965, 1970, and 1975. Imports of these countries account for about 60 percent of world imports.

4 Sterling's Past, Dollar's Future

One can scarcely pick up a financial newspaper without seeing a story about the American dollar's impending loss of international preeminence. This may simply reflect the tendency for financial journalists to find a seat on the nearest bandwagon and ride it for all it is worth. As Mark Twain might have said, reports of the dollar's death have been greatly exaggerated. The dollar is still the dominant reserve currency for the world's central banks and governments. In recent years, the share of international reserves in dollars has actually been rising, not falling. The market in United States treasury securities remains the single most liquid financial market in the world, which makes it attractive for central banks to hold their reserves in this form. The dollar is still the dominant invoicing and vehicle currency in international trade. Petroleum and other commodities are still invoiced in dollars.

There are, of course, good reasons for questioning whether the dollar's dominance will persist. Never before have we seen the extraordinary spectacle of the country issuing the leading international currency running a current account deficit in excess of 6 percent of GDP. Never before have we seen the reserve-currency country in debt to the rest of the world to the extent of 25 percent of its GDP. The connections between America's budget deficits, partly a reflection of the country's overseas military commitments, and the weakness of its currency suggest parallels with the trials of the dollar in the 1960s and with the British pound's tribulations after World War II. All this is bound to raise questions in the minds of those who hold U.S. treasury securities that may lead them to search for alternative forms in which to hold their claims. And for the first time in living memory, there exists another currency, the euro, with a deep and liquid market issued by an economy as large as the United States. Looking forward, there is also the Chinese renminbi, the currency of an economy that fifty years from now may trade even more extensively than the United States does now.

History is widely invoked in discussions of this issue, even by currency forecasters who are typically more comfortable with tick-by-tick data than archival sources. Consider the following quote from Avinash Persaud of State Street Bank and Trust: "Reserve currencies come and go. Over the past two and a half thousand years there have been over a dozen reserve currencies that no longer exist. Sterling lost its status in the first half of the twentieth century, [and] the dollar will lose its status in the first half of this century. . . . Losing reserve currency status will lead to a series of economic and political crises in the United States."[1] While this passage is notable for its pathos, it is not unusual for its history. This is not surprising, for it is necessary to go back in history to find examples of shifts in the identity of the dominant international currency. Indeed, the last time such a shift occurred, from sterling to the dollar, was more than half a century ago. Moreover, if we focus on one specific role of an international currency, as a store of value for the international reserves of central banks and governments, one can argue that this was the only such shift in recorded history.[2] Other monetary units had come in for international use before but not as a form in which to hold liquid paper liabilities in connection with the operation of the international monetary system. Most medieval and early modern examples of "international money" were simply coins that circulated for use across national borders. In the seventeenth and eighteenth centuries, when the Netherlands was a leading international commercial and financial power and Amsterdam was a leading financial center, paper claims became important, but most international operations there were in bills on foreign places, not in claims on the Dutch government itself.[3]

In the remainder of this chapter, I focus on the dollar's role as the world's dominant form for holding official reserves and its place in the international monetary system. There is a sense, therefore, in which we really have only one data point, the transition from sterling to the dollar, from which to draw inferences. Thus, we are truly in the historian's domain.

The History of Reserve-Currency Competition

As I have just suggested, while foreign deposits and purchases of foreign bills and bonds are nothing new, large-scale holdings in foreign financial centers by central banks and governments are a relatively recent development. The spread of this practice coincided with the emergence of the international gold standard in the decades leading up to World War I. With a few important exceptions, the standard in question was a gold bullion standard, not a gold coin standard.[4] A significant share of the monetary circulation of countries on the gold standard was not gold coin, in other words, but token coins and paper convertible into gold bullion under certain circumstances. The gold bullion standard was a nineteenth-century innovation. It presupposed a uniform currency that was difficult to counterfeit, which became possible only when steam power was introduced into the minting process.[5] Once gold was concentrated in the vaults of central banks (or in treasuries and other note-issuing banks when there was no central bank), there was an incentive to substitute or at least augment it with bills and deposit claims that bore interest but were convertible into gold. Peter Lindert's estimates, which nearly four decades after their appearance are still the best available, suggest that foreign exchange rose from a tenth to a seventh of global international reserves between 1880 and 1914.[6]

It is easy enough to understand why London should have been the place where many such reserves were maintained and why sterling bills and deposits should have been their single most important form. Britain was the world's preeminent trading nation, absorbing more than 30 percent of the rest of the world's exports in 1860 and 20 percent in 1890.[7] It was a leading exporter of manufactured goods and services and a voracious consumer of imported foodstuffs and raw materials. Between 1860 and 1914, about 60 percent of world trade was invoiced and settled in sterling.[8] For foreign suppliers seeking to sell, say, cotton, quoting prices in sterling was helpful for breaking into the British market. The supplier would maintain a deposit account in London where receipts could be held safely for short periods. With the growth of imports and reexports of these materials came the development of commodity exchanges where both spot and forward prices were similarly quoted in sterling.[9]

Britain's position as the world's most important source of long-term overseas investment worked in the same direction. Foreign governments seeking to borrow abroad came to London, making sterling the logical unit of account for debt securities, since then as now there was limited appetite for bonds denominated in their own domestic currencies, the markets in which were less liquid and whose value was more easily manipulated by the issuer.[10] When funds became available, it was natural to park them in deposit accounts in London, generally in the same bank that had underwritten the loan.[11] Lenders encouraged the practice on the view that the maintenance of deposits in London was a bonding device that might promote good behavior on the part of the borrower.[12]

Britain's status as an imperial power reinforced sterling's role. From the early eighteenth century, an effort was made to encourage the use of the pound throughout the empire as a way of simplifying and regularizing transactions.[13] British financial institutions established branches in the colonies, and colonial banks opened offices in London. These banks maintained assets and liabilities in London and issued bank notes for the colonies, maintaining a fixed exchange rate between those notes and sterling. When exchange rates misbehaved, the British government imposed direct regulation of local currency issues, requiring full external convertibility of the local currency into sterling at a fixed rate of exchange, something that was maintained by buying and selling sterling on demand in London. In cases like India, where the British sovereign was ultimately made legal tender, the colonial government was led to establish a sizeable reserve in London.

These practices further enhanced the liquidity of the London market, probably the most important fundamental that made it attractive for foreign central banks and governments to hold interest-bearing assets there in the first place. Because the market was deep and liquid, official foreign holders of sterling could augment or deplete their positions without disturbing prices or revealing uncomfortable facts about their balance sheets. They could use sterling to intervene in the foreign exchange market to prevent their exchange rates from straying beyond the gold import and export points. Although problems did arise, these were never of a severity that jeopardized the convertibility of sterling. And while the Bank of England occasionally resorted to the gold devices, modifying the effective price of gold, it never seriously interfered with the freedom of non-Britons to export gold. Few if any other financial centers could claim all of these attributes.[14]

Sterling's preeminence prior to 1914 is frequently invoked as evidence that there can be only one international currency at a given point in time. Then it was the pound, now it is the dollar, and in the future it will be something else. To again quote Persaud, "At any one point in time, there tends to be a single dominant currency in the financial world, not two or more, just one. Some people believe that the euro may not topple the dollar [but that] it will at least share some of the spoils of financial hegemony. History suggests not. In the currency markets the spoils go to the victor, alone; they are not shared."[15]

The notion that there is room in the market for only one reserve currency is based on the concept of network externalities and on the singular dominance of the dollar in the final quarter of the twentieth century.[16] Minimizing

costs, the argument goes, means conducting international transactions in the same currency used by others
for international transactions. As with computer operating systems, there are strong incentives to conform to
the choice that dominates the marketplace.[17] It follows
that one currency tends to be used for the vast majority
of international transactions. The incumbent also tends
to have built-in advantages in maintaining its market
share—in the absence, that is, of a shock sufficiently
large to cause agents to shift all at once to another
standard.[18]

This argument may carry some weight in the choice of
currency for invoicing trade or denominating foreign
debt securities, but it is less obviously valid for the currency denomination of reserves.[19] It may pay to hold
reserves in the most liquid market, which tends to be the
market in which everyone else holds reserves, but there
is no reason to assume, in general, that only one market
can possess adequate liquidity. In addition, market liquidity is not the only thing that matters. It may be worth
tolerating a bit less market liquidity in return for the benefits of greater diversification or as an expression of good
faith to the investment bank that one seeks to have
underwrite one's loans. And if there is no strong network
externality encouraging one to hold reserves in the same
currency as other central banks, then there is no lock-in to
prevent central banks from altering the currency composition of their reserve portfolios in response to new information about expected gains and losses.

Nor is the historical evidence obviously consistent with the notion that the spoils go to the victor alone. At the end of 1913, sterling balances accounted for less than half of the total official foreign exchange holdings whose currency of denomination is known, while French francs accounted for perhaps a third and German marks a sixth (see table 4.1).[20] Over the preceding quarter century, sterling's share had in fact been falling, not rising, mainly in consequence of the growing share of the French franc. In Europe itself, sterling was a distant third as a form in which to hold official reserves, behind both the franc and the mark.

Neither is interwar experience obviously consistent with the notion that one currency dominates international usage. In the 1920s and 1930s, three currencies shared this role, although the dollar had now supplanted the mark. The establishment of the Federal Reserve System in 1914 enhanced the liquidity of the New York

Table 4.1
Shares of currencies in known official foreign exchange assets, 1899 to 1913

	End of 1899	End of 1913
Sterling	64	48
Francs	16	31
Marks	15	15
Other currencies	6	6

Source: Calculated from Lindert (1969, table 3).

Notes: Percentages may not sum to 100 due to rounding.

market and heightened its attractions as an international financial center.[21] Before World War I, the dollar had scarcely been used in international transactions.[22] There was no American central bank to rediscount dollar acceptances, purchase dollar-denominated bills, and otherwise ensure the liquidity of the market. All this changed, of course, with the founding of the Federal Reserve.

World War I had a reinforcing effect. Germany suspended convertibility in the opening week of the war. The Bank of France, which had never been legally obliged to convert notes into gold, did so only under exceptional circumstances before an official gold embargo was imposed in 1915. Britain restricted the export and melting of gold in 1917. The United States, in contrast, preserved gold convertibility even after it entered the war in 1917.[23]

Reflecting the operation of the beachhead effect, American shares of global trade and foreign lending were then markedly higher in the 1920s than they had been before World War I.[24] In turn, this led to an expansion in the dollar's role as a unit of account and means of payment for international transactions between private parties. Germany and France suffered financial turmoil in the first half of the 1920s. In the second half of the decade, the Bank of England was continuously "under the harrow," in Montagu Norman's famous phrase.[25]

And yet, despite all this, sterling, the dollar, and the franc shared reserve-currency status in the 1920s and 1930s. We still lack careful Lindert-like estimates of the relative shares of the three currencies. But sterling was probably still first, followed by the dollar and the franc.[26]

The conventional wisdom that one currency dominates reserve holdings worldwide thus derives almost entirely from the second half of the twentieth century, when the greenback accounted for as much as 85 percent of global foreign-exchange reserves (see table 4.2). In part, the post–World War II hegemony of the dollar reflected the exceptional dominance by the United States of global trade and payments in a period when Europe and Japan had not yet fully recovered from the aftermath of World War II and modern economic growth had yet to spread to what we now refer to as developing countries.[27] In addition, the dollar's hegemony reflected the fact that the governments of other potential reserve centers actively discouraged the international use of their currencies. Germany saw internationalization of the deutschemark as a threat to its control of inflation. Japan saw the internationalization of the yen as incompatible with its system of directed credit. France had seen more than once how allowing private foreign funds to move in might also allow them to move out if investors concluded that the government's macroeconomic policy aspirations were incompatible with its stated commitment to currency stability. These and other considerations led the countries whose currencies were potential rivals to the dollar to maintain significant capital controls well into the post–World War II period, in some cases until the end of the 1980s. These controls in turn limited the liquidity of their securities markets, which made financial assets denominated in their currencies less attractive as a form of reserves. Thus, it was not just the unusually large size of the United States in the world economy or the admirable liquidity of American financial markets but the maintenance of controls by other potential reserve centers that explains why the dollar was so dominant as a reserve currency for so long after World War II. While most of these controls were relaxed or removed by the 1990s, this decade was marked by a slump in Japan and Europe's uncertain transition to the euro, making it an inauspicious time for radical portfolio reallocation.[28] In addition, the rapid growth of the American economy, especially in the second half of the 1990s, meant that the dollar's dominance troubled few reserve managers. The question now is whether this sanguine view might change.

Some might argue that once gained, reserve-currency status is hard to lose. Is not the persistence of sterling's reserve-currency role into the second half of the twentieth century, long after the United Kingdom's international commercial and financial preeminence had passed, evidence of this? I am not convinced. After World War II, sterling reserves were held not so much because of any lingering incentives conferred by network externalities but mainly as a matter of loyalty by members of the Commonwealth and by British colonies with limited choice in the matter.[29] It is not clear that America's "informal empire" will command similar loyalty among the central banks of Asia and the Middle East.

Table 4.2
Currency composition of foreign exchange reserves (percentage)

Regime	1973	1987	1995	2004
U.S. dollar	84.5	66.0	56.4	65.9
Euro	—	—	—	24.9
Sterling	5.9	2.2	2.1	3.3
German mark	6.7	13.4	15.8	—
French franc	1.2	0.8	2.4	—
Swiss franc	1.4	1.5	0.3	0.2
Yen	—	7.0	6.8	3.9
ECU	—	5.7	8.5	—
Other	—	3.4	4.8	1.8

Source: IMF, Annual Report (various years).

In addition to loyalty, another reason that members of the sterling area were reluctant to diversify their reserves out of the pound more quickly was that they recognized that doing so might aggravate the problems of the British economy, on which they depended as an export market. They valued the exchange-rate and financial stability conferred by the greater sterling area and were reluctant to precipitate its break-up.[30] Their position became less tenable following the 1967 devaluation, as a result of which capital losses were once more imposed on sterling-area countries. This led to negotiation of the Basel Facility of 1968 and the associated bilateral agreements in which the United Kingdom guaranteed the value in dollars of the official sterling reserves of sterling-area countries, in return for which each partner country pledged not to reduce its official sterling balances beyond a certain point. Now, of course, the United States is not inclined to extend a similar guarantee.

What about the fact that the American liquid liabilities held by foreign central banks are large relative to the foreign liquid assets of the Federal Reserve and the government of the United States? Doesn't this heighten the likelihood of a shift into alternative reserve assets? By itself, history suggests, this fact is not a threat to the reserve-currency status of the dollar. In 1913, the liquid sterling claims held by official foreign institutions were 2.5 times greater than the Bank of England's gold reserves.[31] After 1959, official foreign holdings of dollars similarly exceeded the gold reserves of the United States.[32] In both instances, there was talk of the difficulties that would arise if foreign creditors suddenly decided to liquidate these claims. But in neither case did wholesale liquidation occur, and in neither case was the status of the reserve currency seriously threatened. In each instance, the accumulation of liquid claims on the reserve-currency country was a natural corollary of that country's status as a financial center and of the rising demand for reserves created by a growing world economy.

One hears the same reassuring argument today. It is said that the United States is borrowing short and lending long because it has a more efficient financial system and because the countries on the other side of the intermediation process have voracious appetites for liquid foreign reserves.[33] China buys liquid claims on the United

States in the form of American treasury securities, and the United States turns around and uses the proceeds to fund less liquid foreign direct investment in China, circumventing the inefficiencies of the Chinese banking system. This is simply an updating of the Emile Despres, Charles Kindleberger, and Walter Salant view of the American balance of payments in the 1960s.[34] Recall that Despres, Kindleberger, and Salant argued that it was misleading to focus on balance-of-payments statistics that put net long-term foreign assets above the line but not short-term foreign assets below it when both components were in fact parts of the same intermediation process.[35] Of course, the same was also the case before 1914, when Britain borrowed short and lent long, acting as banker to the world.[36] If there was no particular reason to worry at that time about liquid claims of foreign official creditors that exceeded liquid foreign assets, it is said, then it follows that there is no reason to worry now.

But there is a difference between these two previous episodes and today—namely, that the present situation occurs against the backdrop of large, ongoing current-account deficits for the country that is banker to the world. In principle, there is no reason that the country with the most efficient financial system that is providing intermediation services to the world cannot run a balanced current account or even a surplus. There is no reason that importing short-term capital and exporting long-term capital should require the banker to the world to run a current account deficit, as the United States is

doing.[37] America ran current account surpluses following World War II, even after contemporaries stopped
referring to the dollar gap. Similarly, Britain ran persistent current account surpluses before World War I.[38]

Advocates of this banker-to-the-world view argue that
other countries are running surpluses against the United
States and accumulating reserves in the form of dollars
because these serve as collateral for U.S. foreign direct
investment.[39] American corporations are willing to build
factories in China, according to this view, because they
know that if the Chinese authorities attempt to expropri-
ate them, the government of the United States will freeze
China's dollar reserves. In the nineteenth century, gun-
boats provided this function. After World War II, the
United States' nuclear umbrella did the same. Now it is
the balance of financial terror.[40]

I do not find this rationale for being complacent about
America's twin deficits very compelling. The story is
China specific, but the accumulation of reserves and
chronic surpluses with the United States are pan-Asian.
And no one worries that Japan or South Korea will expro-
priate American investments. I am not aware of American
corporate executives who have pointed to China's large
dollar reserves as a form of collateral in justifying their
decision to invest there. Nor am I aware of statements by
Chinese officials where they explain that they are accumulating U.S. treasuries as a way of posting collateral for
foreign direct investment inflows. Moreover, the timing
is wrong: U.S. foreign direct investments in China rose

starting around 1992, whereas the massive reserve accumulation came only a decade later. Given the difficulty of identifying the final holders of American treasury securities, it is not clear that selective default of this sort is feasible. And given that the United States accounts for only a small fraction of foreign direct investment in China, one must assume that the United States would be willing to compromise its public-credit standing in this way not just on behalf of American private foreign investors but also on behalf of those from other countries. Historically, the way that foreign investments in China have been expropriated is through the surreptitious stripping of assets by Chinese managers and joint-venture partners. It is hard to imagine that the government of the United States would risk tarnishing its public credit in response to more such instances. Rather, one has to assume a major geopolitical blow-up between the United States and China, a decision by Beijing to freeze all American investments there, and retaliation by the American government in the form of freezing Chinese treasury bond holdings. Such events are not beyond all realm of possibility, but these do not strike me as the obvious way of explaining the current pattern of global imbalances.

In my view, the fact that the reserve-currency country is running large current account deficits and is incurring a rapidly growing net foreign debt threatens to undermine its position as banker to the world. It means that long-term foreign claims on the United States are as easily liquefied as long-term American claims on

foreigners—even more so to the extent that long-term
American foreign assets take the form of illiquid foreign
direct investment and the country's long-term foreign
liabilities take the form of U.S. treasury bonds. While
there may be something to the "banker to the world"
metaphor, now—unlike Britain before 1914 and the
United States before 1971—we are talking about a bank
with negative net capital.

A modest net foreign debt may not be a problem, given
the strength of the American economy and its attractions
for foreign investors. The United States has other sources
of strength, not just its financial capital. But if its outstanding debt is allowed to grow relative to GDP, sooner
or later foreigners will grow reluctant to hold more dollars and dollar-denominated assets. This reluctance
could lead to currency depreciation and inflation in the
United States that ultimately makes holding reserves in
dollars less attractive.

Michael Mussa provides a simple way of thinking
about this. Mussa shows that the ratio of net foreign liabilities to GDP, denoted n, stabilizes when $c = n * g$, where
c is the current account deficit as a share of GDP and g is
the rate of growth of nominal income.[41] If g is 0.05 (3 percent real growth plus 2 percent inflation) and c is 0.025,
then the debt ratio stabilizes at 50 percent, double the
current 25 percent and perhaps the plausible upper
bound on how much American net debt foreigners might
be willing to hold. (This is also what Mussa assumes,
with some caveats. It will be useful for what follows to

assume that inflation in the rest of the world also runs at
2 percent, the upper bound of the ECB's target range.)[42]
Assume now that the United States does nothing to
raise its public and household savings rates and that the
current account deficit is allowed to continue running at
5 percent of GDP. With $g = 0.05$ and $c = 0.05$, the debt ratio
now stabilizes at 100 percent.[43] This is a much higher
ratio than has ever been incurred by a large country,
much less by a reserve-currency country. It implies that
foreigners would have to hold a considerably greater
share of their portfolios than at present in the form of
claims on the United States. This result, in other words, is
implausible. Something has to give.

One way of squaring the circle, assuming no change in
c, which is what we are assuming for the moment, is to
raise the rate of inflation from, say, 2 to 7 percent, with
the result that the rate of nominal income growth rises
from 5 to 10 percent.[44] With $c = 0.05$ and $g = .10$, n again stabilizes at 50 percent, which we are assuming to be the
upper bound. The most likely way in which this would
come about is that foreigners would grow unwilling to add
more dollar-denominated securities to their portfolios.
Keeping the share of dollar-denominated securities in foreign portfolios constant, even while the United States continues to pump additional treasury bonds into the world
economy, requires the dollar's exchange rate to fall.[45] And
once it begins falling, there may be a "rush out of dollars,"
as investors scramble to avoid ending up holding the bag
(to avoid incurring large capital losses as a result of being

late). And the faster the dollar drops, the greater are imported inflation and upward pressure on U.S. price levels. This is how market forces produce the acceleration in inflation that limits the rise in the American external— debt-to-GNP ratio to levels acceptable to investors.

Some will object that the Federal Reserve would not be prepared to countenance a significant acceleration of inflation. They have in mind that it would raise interest rates sharply to damp down incipient inflationary pressure. Whether this provides a smooth way out depends on how we think the Fed's higher interest rates will affect the U.S. economy and the current account. Sharply higher interest rates would depress both absorption and output.[46] This would slow consumer spending through its negative impact on house prices and the value of other assets and depress investment by raising the cost of capital. Higher interest rates would depress the growth of output through their negative effects on investment and aggregate demand generally. If the main item that falls is absorption, then the current account will narrow, and portfolio equilibrium can be restored without rapid inflation. But if the main variable that falls is production, then the current account (being the difference between absorption and production) may show little improvement. Higher interest rates that depress output may then also destabilize the financial system. After all, the combination of higher interest rates and a collapsing exchange rate, occurring against the backdrop of chronic fiscal and external imbalances, is the classic recipe for a financial crisis.

None of these scenarios has happy implications for the dollar's role as the world's leading reserve currency. Assume first that the Federal Reserve does not attempt to offset the inflationary effects of the falling dollar. With the American inflation rate now running at three times the inflation rate in other countries, using the dollar as a store of value and a vehicle and invoicing currency would become less attractive.[47] The resulting capital losses would eventually encourage foreign central banks and governments to find a more stable repository for their reserves.[48] Alternatively, assume that the Federal Reserve raises the discount rate sharply to prevent an acceleration of inflation. This might precipitate a sharp recession and financial distress and potentially an even sharper drop in the dollar. Again this would lead foreign central banks and other holders to shift out of dollars to avoid capital losses.[49] Only if we assume that the Fed can engineer a soft landing—that it can raise interest rates just enough to contain inflation but without precipitating a serious recession and thereby reduce c after all—would there be a smooth way out.

Future Prospects

What does this scenario imply for the dollar's place at the center of the global financial system? It implies that whether the dollar retains its reserve-currency role depends, first and foremost, on America's own policies. Serious economic mismanagement would lead to the

substitution of other reserve currencies for the dollar. By
"serious mismanagement," I mean policies that allow
unsustainably large current account deficits to persist,
lead to the accumulation of large external debts, and
culminate in a disorderly adjustment process involving
dollar depreciation and either a sharp increase in
domestic inflation rates or a sharp fall in the nominal
value of American debt securities due to higher interest
rates. Clearly, instability of the dollar exchange rate and
the erosion of the purchasing power of dollar-denominated assets would make holding dollar reserves unattractive. This is a lesson of British history in that an
inflation rate that ran at roughly three times U.S. rates
over the first three quarters of the twentieth century, in
conjunction with repeated devaluations against the dollar, played a major role in sterling's loss of international
preeminence.

In the more optimistic scenario in which the American
current account deficit is gradually brought under control,
there is no reason why the dollar should lose its reserve-
currency status, given the stability of the United States'
monetary policy, its vibrant economy, and the liquidity of
American financial markets. But this does not mean that
the dollar will remain as dominant on the international
stage as it has been in the past. As financial markets
elsewhere in the world gain liquidity, other currencies
will become more convenient forms in which to hold
reserves. For more than four decades after World War II,
other countries maintained capital controls and tight

financial regulations that limited the liquidity of their markets, rendering their currencies less attractive as repositories for reserves and perpetuating the dominance of the dollar. Now, with financial normalization and liberalization, some diversification out of dollars is inevitable. This does not mean that the dollar is doomed to lose its reserve-currency status. The network-externalities argument that competition for reserve-currency status is a winner-take-all game holds little water either analytically or historically. Looking forward, financial innovation will continue to reduce the costs of converting currencies, further weakening the incentive to hold reserves in the same form that other countries hold reserves simply to minimize transactions costs. Thus, there is no reason why, several decades from now, two or more reserve currencies cannot share the market, not unlike the situation before 1914.

But which currencies? The obvious candidates, whether we are thinking of 2020 or 2040, are the dollar and the euro. Europe and the United States have strong institutions, respect for property rights, and sound macroeconomic policies relative to the rest of the world. These countries have stable political systems. Their economies are likely to be of roughly equal size, to engage in similar levels of external trade and financial transactions, and to have comparably liquid securities markets. The advent of the euro has done much to increase the liquidity of European bond markets, which is critical from the point of view of enhancing reserve-currency status.

All this is predicated on the assumption of a healthy European economy and a euro area that holds together. If economic growth in Europe continues to lag economic growth in the United States and Asia, Europe will come to figure less importantly on the global economic and financial scene. The euro will be rendered more of a specialized currency like the Swiss franc, useful for diversifying reserve holdings, rather than used as a major constituent of central bank portfolios. Moreover, Europe remains a heterogeneous place. That is to say, if some European countries conclude that the policies of the European Central Bank are too tight for their liking, they could conceivably be tempted to defect from the euro area and to reintroduce their own national currencies. In this scenario, in which only a hard core of EU member states retains the euro, that currency would again resemble the Swiss franc more than the American dollar in terms of its reserve-currency role.

Personally, I do not regard this as a likely scenario. Monetary union is one of a set of related bargains reached by the members of the European Union. It is hard to break one such agreement without jeopardizing the others, a fact that constitutes a formidable barrier to exit. Moreover, it is not clear that a country like Italy, for example, would really be better off with its own currency and a more expansionary monetary policy.[50] The main effect of reintroducing the lira might be to raise the cost of servicing its national debt, which hardly makes this option desirable. Finally, not everyone would agree that the prospects for growth are fundamentally inferior in Europe compared to the United States.[51] But the scenario is still worth considering for those contemplating the medium-term prospects of the euro as a reserve currency.

The other popular candidates for reserve currency status are not likely to be major rivals to the dollar. Japan is a smaller country with a demographic problem and a resistance to immigration. Absent a dramatic revival in growth and a fundamental shift in immigration policies, its place on the global landscape will continue to shrink over time. Everyone's favorite heir to the throne, China, will have to surmount significant hurdles before its currency begins to become attractive as a repository for other countries' foreign exchange reserves. Figuring out how to remove capital controls without destabilizing the economy is the least of its problems. China's financial markets are not very liquid or transparent; indeed, most of the institutional infrastructure needed for Shanghai to become a true international financial center will take decades to install. The security of property rights is uncertain, and making investors feel secure will ultimately require a transition to democracy, the creation of credible political checks and balances, and the development of a creditor class with political sway. While the renminbi is many people's favorite candidate for the new reserve-currency champion four or five decades from now, such hopes, in my opinion, are highly premature.

My message is that history must be read carefully. In fact, several currencies can share reserve-currency status, as they not infrequently have. Changes in financial technologies and market structures, which weaken network effects, make it even more likely that this will be true in the future than the past. At the same time, mistaken policies can quickly knock a currency out of contention. Time will tell whether this fate befalls the dollar.

Notes

Preface

1. None of the views expressed are necessarily those of the Bank of Japan.

Chapter 1

1. See Dooley, Folkerts-Landau, and Garber (2003).

2. Some would include Latin America as part of the new periphery. Argentina in particular seems to have committed to a process of export-led growth predicated on an undervalued exchange rate.

3. In chapter 3 below, the comparison between China and Japan is made explicit.

4. In Eichengreen (1996b).

5. See, e.g., Ohkawa and Rosovsky (1973).

6. One way to calculate European and Japanese real exchange rates in this period is to convert European and Japanese wages into dollars at the prevailing nominal rate and compare them with U.S. wages. This reminds us that wage restraint and undervalued exchange rates are simply two sides of the same coin. For more on this, see chapter 3.

7. On this aspect of the comparison, see BIS (2005, pp. 180 et seq.).

8. The Gold Pool, made up of Belgium, France, Germany, Italy, the Netherlands, Switzerland, the United Kingdom, and the United States, is the subject of chapter 2.

9. The United States having demonetized gold in 1934.

10. By "carefully unspecified conditions," I mean that a conscious decision was taken not to define the meaning of the term "fundamental disequilibrium" determining the circumstances under which a parity could be changed.

11. See Keynes (1944).

12. Gourinchas and Rey (2005) note that the phrase "exorbitant privilege" appears nowhere in de Gaulle's speeches but is properly attributable to Valéry Giscard d'Estaing, French finance minister in 1965.

13. The only noteworthy revaluations of the period were those of Germany and the Netherlands in 1961 and Germany in 1969.

14. U.S. direct military expenditures abroad rose sharply after 1965. The deterioration of the balance on government account was almost a mirror image.

15. The classic statement of the problem from the French perspective was Servan-Schreiber (1967).

16. See Block (1977).

17. The quote is from the fourth Kennedy-Nixon debate (21 October 1960).

18. "First, we pledge ourselves to maintain the current value of the dollar. If elected President I shall not devalue the dollar from the present rate. Rather I shall defend the present value and its soundness," spoke candidate Kennedy in Philadelphia on 31 October 1960 (Roosa 1967, p. 268). There is a strong dollar policy if I have ever heard one.

19. Opting to raise the dollar price of gold would have also politicized subsequent decisions, since the administration would have had to go to the Congress for approval to raise the $35-an-ounce price.

20. See Meltzer (1966).

21. See Shultz and Dam (1977) and Gowa (1983). Nixon's import surcharge, however regrettable on other grounds, provided the United

States with a bargaining chip that could be used to discourage other countries from following the United States dollar for dollar. But the problem with the import surcharge, besides the threat posed to the world trading system, was that it greatly complicated efforts to cooperate in good faith on redesign of the international monetary system. Here, again, is a suggestive parallel with the current situation in which congressional critics of Chinese currency policy have threatened the imposition of a 27.5 percent tariff on merchandise imports from that country.

22. This is the conclusion pointed to by the simulation model developed and analyzed in Bordo and Eichengreen (1998).

23. This implies that the day of reckoning would have been delayed even less than suggested by the second of these two counterfactuals.

24. On those rare occasions when the Fed did tighten and the executive and legislative branches did agree on a tax hike, as in 1968, the balance of payments recovered, but economic growth suffered. And the counterreaction was intense.

25. Operation Twist involved attempting to twist the yield curve by selling short-term treasury bills while buying long-term bonds and thus to stimulate domestic investment with lower long-term rates while attracting capital inflows with higher short-term yields (see Meltzer 1991).

26. This phraseology is designed to be consistent with the fact that U.S. wholesale and consumer price inflation was generally lower than inflation in other industrial countries but was insufficiently so for the maintenance of external balance, given rapid catch-up growth (and the operation of the Balassa-Samuelson effect) in these other countries.

27. For example, in Working Party 3 of the OECD's Economic Policy Committee (see Roosa 1967).

28. See Roosa (1967). It is revealing that Kennedy had proposed U.S. membership in his balance-of-payments message (a special message to the Congress on the balance of payments delivered on 6 February 1961, barely three weeks after the new president took office).

29. These data were then circulated among the members of the G-10 and to Working Party 3 of the OECD on a confidential basis.

30. Toniolo (2005, p. 378).

31. Only ASEAN has a modest permanent secretariat.

32. The idea of the Asian Bond Fund (ABF), launched by the Executives' Meeting of East Asia-Pacific Central Banks (EMEAP) in June 2003, is to catalyze the growth of Asian bond markets by allocating a portion of the reserves of regional central banks to purchases of government and quasi-government securities. The initial round of $1 billion of investments, known as ABF-1, was devoted exclusively to Asian sovereign and quasi-sovereign issuers' dollar-denominated bonds. The Asian Bond Markets Initiative was endorsed by ASEAN+3 finance ministers at their meeting in Manila, the Philippines, in August 2003 with the goals of the ABMI to foster an active and liquid secondary market in local-currency bonds and to develop the infrastructure needed for the growth of local bond markets.

33. ABF-2 was announced in December 2004 to invest in domestic-currency sovereign and quasi-sovereign bonds in eight EMEAP markets. Investments are projected to amount to roughly $2 billion and will be administered by the BIS.

34. This dilemma is the subject of chapter 2 below.

35. Which would have thereby increased the pressure on the latter to convert their dollar overhang into gold.

36. As noted by Garber (1993).

37. See Eichengreen (2005).

38. For more on this, see chapter 3.

39. The example is not entirely reassuring, since it first led to a crisis in a credit-card industry. The banks have now installed new management teams that have insisted on more rigorous controls, such that their consumer lending is now highly profitable (see Moon 2005).

40. See, however, the discussion of the euro's uncertain prospects in chapter 4 below.

Chapter 2

1. See Solomon (1977).

2. A prominent exception is the recently published history of the BIS by Toniolo (2005).

3. Contemporaries referred to a "conspiracy of silence" regarding the operation of the pool. See, inter alia, Louchheim (1968).

4. This is the basic message of the literature on speculative attacks (e.g., Henderson and Salant 1978; Krugman 1979; Flood and Garber 1984).

5. One implication of the hybrid nature of the system was the pervasive disagreement about how to refer to it—as a gold-exchange standard or a gold-dollar standard (see, e.g., Gilbert 1968).

6. See, for example, Triffin (1947).

7. Between 1953 and 1967, the U.S. wholesale price index rose by 16 percent, while the dollar price of gold rose not at all.

8. There were also IMF quotas, of course, which permitted greater efficiency via pooling of the gold reserves that countries paid in as their gold tranche. Eventually, there were also Special Drawing Rights, although these came too late to affect the fate of the Gold Pool (see chapter 1).

9. The actual intervention price was $35.20, the official $35.08 U.S. price plus the costs of shipping and insurance of getting gold to London.

10. Or they could simply hold it, enjoying the option value of being able to sell it at that higher price at a future date.

11. Solomon (1968, pp. 5–6).

12. Capital controls and other restrictive regulations helped to bottle up these pressures. This is one reason that the distinction between official and private holdings and, for that matter, between foreign and domestic claims on the U.S. government mattered in the first place. But those controls and restrictive regulations worked imperfectly.

13. See chapter 1.

14. This was not the first time such an idea had been mooted. Governor Brunet of the Bank of France had suggested something similar in November 1960 in response to the effects of the U.S. presidential election, but other countries were unwilling to proceed except at U.S. initiative. See Toniolo (2005, pp. 375 et seq.).

15. Precise shares were 50 percent for the United States, 11 percent for West Germany, 9¼ each percent for France, Italy, and the United Kingdom, and 3¾ percent each for Belgium, the Netherlands, and Switzerland.

16. See "Memorandum by Alfred Hayes," 16 November 1961, U.S. Treasury Papers, Box 108, RG 56-97-60-25, U.S. National Archives.

17. On France's defection from the Gold Pool, see the next section below.

18. See "The Future of Gold Pool Operations," July 1966, U.S. Treasury Papers, Box 29, RG56-450-80-24-01, U.S. National Archives.

19. Market prices rose for short periods such as during the Cuban crisis, but these were exceptions to the rule.

20. "Taking the Fun Out" (1964, p. 132).

21. Toniolo (2005, chap. 11, p. 414).

22. See "The London Gold Crisis 1968," PRO T267/21 (January 1975), p. 11.

23. Solomon (1977, p. 115). This was also the reaction of T. P. Nelson in a memo to the Treasury Secretary, 29 November 1967, p. 1. Treasury Papers, Box 29, 69A-75-84-29, U.S. National Archives.

24. And the next week, the *Wall Street Journal* reported that American businessmen and tourists were buying gold in Mexico City in violation of statutes barring Americans from holding gold. The U.S. Treasury concluded that these reports were exaggerated, but the damage to confidence had been done. See J. P. Hendrick, "Investigation of Gold Regulations Violations," 8 December 1967, Treasury Papers, Box 29, 69A-75-84-29, U.S. National Archives.

25. In addition, they agreed to propose legislation designed to abolish the 25 percent gold cover on Federal Reserve notes, thus making more of its reserve available to meet the demands of foreign central banks. See below.

26. Italy reportedly sought guarantees from the United States that it would be compensated for in the event that it made further contributions to the Gold Pool and if the dollar price of gold then rose further.

27. T. P. Nelson, "Gold Market Outlook," Confidential Memorandum to Under Secretary Deming, 16 March, U.S. Treasury Papers, Box 29, RG56-450-80-24-01, U.S. National Archives.

28. See "A Gold Certificate Plan to Stabilize the Gold Market," 24 November 1967, U.S. Treasury Papers, Box 29, RG56-450-80-24-01, U.S. National Archives. European objections to the Gold Certificate Plan (ascribed principally to Ansiaux and Carli) are detailed in "Reactions to the Certificate Plan," 10 February 1968, U.S. Treasury Papers, Box 29, RG56-450-80-24-01, U.S. National Archives.

29. Quoted in *New York Times*, 12 March 1968, p. 66.

30. In addition, until early 1965 a 25 percent gold reserve was required against Federal Reserve Bank deposits. The parallel with the problem of free gold in 1931 was direct (Eichengreen 1992). The issue is not whether the constraint actually bound (in neither case did it) or whether it could be relaxed by legislative action or decree (in each case it could) but whether market participants had doubts about these matters and those doubts in turn ratcheted up the pressure on the Fed. See Solomon (1977, p. 117).

31. "The Development of Central Bank Co-operation," 28 November 1963, BIS Archive File 7 18(16), Box HAL 2, Folder 01.

32. The mechanics of this process are set out by Genberg and Swoboda (1993).

33. Just how deflationary consequences would have been avoided in this scenario was never entirely clear. The French certainly did not have in mind a shift to generalized floating and the demonetization of gold that occurred after 1971. Nor were they enthusiastic supporters of the creation of a synthetic reserve asset, given their commitment to gold.

34. See Frankel and Rockett (1988) and Eichengreen and Uzan (1993).

35. Robert Solomon, then working for the Federal Reserve Board, recognized this problem and proposed linking the continuation of the Gold Pool with the creation of a new reserve asset (along the lines of what eventually became the SDR). As it happened, the collapse of the Gold Pool and the creation of a two-tier gold market in 1968 with one price (the London market price) for private transactions and a

second price ($35 an ounce) for official transactions did help to restore equilibrium after a fashion. The rise in the market price created an incentive for South Africa to expand its gold production and sales, eventually driving the market price back down to $35. But this response occurred only after the official and market prices of gold were decoupled, and it took a considerable period of time to operate. This was precisely how the maintenance of price stability was supposed to work under the classical gold standard. (For a modern statement of the mechanism, see Barro 1979.) Under the classical gold standard as well, the problem was that the induced response of the gold mining industry took a considerable period of time to operate (Eichengreen 1996a). In the meantime, the signals sent by the divergence of the two prices reminded central banks of the incentives to hedge their bets.

36. Memorandum from Mr. Widman to Under Secretary Deming, 21 January, Box 56, U.S. Treasury Papers, 69A 75-84-29.

37. "World War I Debts and Gold Conversion," 19 February 1968, Box 28, U.S. Treasury Papers, 69A 75-84-28.

38. "Gold Pool's First Years," 1962, pp. 1293–1294, cited in Toniolo (2005, p. 380).

39. Would the world have been better off had the Gold Pool never existed? The answer depends on one's view of how events would have played out in its absence. Would the United States have responded with monetary and fiscal consolidation to limit its loss of gold? Would this have resulted in deflationary pressure on the world economy and caused countries short on reserves to slap controls on imports and financial transactions? Alternatively, would the United States have been quicker to close the gold window? If so, might this have led to an earlier transition to generalized floating? Or might the prospect of a generalized crisis have accelerated the negotiation and issuance of an alternative, synthetic form of reserves—what eventually became Special Drawing Rights? Might this have sustained the system of pegged but adjustable exchange rates into the 1970s and beyond? These are important and interesting counterfactuals, but they are properly the subject of a separate study.

40. Truman (2005).

Chapter 3

1. The 1913 to 1950 figure is depressed by the exceptional events of the post–World War II period. Over the shorter period 1913 to 1940, growth averaged 4.0 percent.

2. This nearly matches rates of export growth in China, which have been running on the order of 20 percent per annum in recent years.

3. This according to Ohkawa and Rosovsky (1973).

4. That widespread underemployment was more than a transitory post–World War II phenomenon is evident in the rationale for the famous National Income Doubling Plan of 1960, which was precisely to reduce the extent of disguised unemployment. Prime Minister Hayato Ikeda announced the Income Doubling Plan immediately after he took office in 1960. The plan was crystallized as a cabinet decision in December 1960 (Yasuba and Inoki 1989, p. 18). Its primary goals were a sharp improvement in living standards and the achievement of full employment. The plan intended to achieve an annual average growth of 7.2 percent between fiscal year of 1961 and 1966. To reach that target, the following areas were given priority: improvement of social infrastructure and industrial structure, enhancement of trade and international economic cooperation, and stimulating technology and human resources (Kosai 1989, pp. 210–212).

5. More precisely, Ohkawa and Rosovsky (1973) suggest that wages in large industrial enterprises were as much as twice wages in small and medium-size firms, while wages in the modern sector broadly defined (small and large firms alike) were twice the levels prevailing in agriculture.

6. According to estimates in Maddison (2001, table C3-c).

7. Mason (1992); Kosai (1989) points out that one of the reasons for restricting inward FDI was the fear that this would hamper domestic research and development.

8. To put it another way, one rationale for maintaining an undervalued exchange rate is to offset another distortion (rural underemployment) that makes the social returns to employment in the modern export-oriented sector much higher than the returns to employment in the

rural sector. See Dooley, Folkerts-Landau, and Garber (2003). Since China today has more rural underemployment, it can be argued that it should avoid further revaluation. On the other hand, this argument for sticking to an undervalued rate to accelerate the movement of rural labor to the modern sector makes no sense when the authorities are at the same time attempting to limit internal migration for fear of social dislocations.

9. Discount rates applied to BOJ lending to private banks (discounts and loans on bills). From 1946 to 1963, the BOJ applied discount rates to predetermined amounts of BOJ lending and amounts over the ceiling were subject to higher interest rates. By changing the level of the ceiling, the BOJ could affect the lending behavior of banks.

10. From 1949 to 1956, the BOJ influenced corporate bond issuance by determining the eligibility of bonds for use as collateral. Financial intermediaries, mainly banks, purchased about 90 percent of corporate bonds, and those bonds were immediately passed to the BOJ as collateral for BOJ lending. When monetary conditions eased in the mid-1950s, the banks' dependence on BOJ lending declined, and the BOJ's de facto power through this mechanism disappeared. After the pre-issue examination of eligibility was eliminated, eight major banks, including Industrial Bank of Japan and the major city banks, developed informal arrangements whereby they determined detailed conditions for corporate-bond issuance in conjunction with the BOJ. Thus, the central bank continued to exercise considerable influence over the volume of issuance (Japan Ministry of Finance 1991b, pp. 570–572; Association of Public and Corporate Bond Underwriters 1980, pp. 232–233, 239).

11. Japan Ministry of Finance (1991a, p. 87). From 1948 to 1957, the BOJ "guided" market participants to trade at a particular overnight interest rate in the call market. This de facto regulation of call-loan interest rates was abolished in 1957, but self-imposed controls by financial institutions were adopted two years later. The effectiveness of the self-imposed controls was not satisfactory, and the actual interest rates applied to transactions were higher than published rates. Thus, the BOJ again started to "guide" call loan brokers in 1962, and in the mid-1960s this control gradually moved toward a quotation system under which call-loan brokers decided quoted prices with the consultation to the BOJ (Japan Ministry of Finance 1991a, pp. 89, 111, 155–158).

12. Japan Ministry of Finance (1991a, p. 313).

13. There is some controversy over this. Authors like Mikuni and Murphy (2002) suggest that the banks came under strong moral suasion to plow their loans into capital formation in export industries in particular. Others, like Horiuchi (1984), are more skeptical that the authorities were able to influence the allocation of bank lending in this way.

14. Estimates of the extent of nonperforming loans in China are on the order of 40 to 50 percent of GDP.

15. Joseph M. Dodge, the president of Detroit Bank, was appointed envoy to the general headquarters of the occupying forces. For details of the Dodge Line, see Nakamura (2003) and Miwa (2003).

16. Odaka (1989, pp. 175–176, authors' translation) writes in a representative passage that "it should not be neglected that the fixed exchange rate of 360 yen against dollar was firmly kept until 1972 and that this was behind the export expansion."

17. For references, see Nakamura (1993, pp. 137 et seq). An analysis of this phenomenon is Ackley and Ishi (1976).

18. Note the similarity to recent discussions of China.

19. Japan Ministry of Finance (1976, pp. 430–431; Bank of Japan (1985, pp. 255–256).

20. Bank of Japan (1985, p. 258, author's translation).

21. Komiya (1988, p. 160, author's translation).

22. Kosai (1989, p. 265).

23. See, inter alia, Fujino (1988) and Kosai (1989).

24. On this, see Kojima (1972).

25. Shinohara (1959, p. 24).

26. Ackley and Ishi (1976, p. 187) note that the 1963 to 1964 and 1966 to 1970 cyclical expansions were the first ones that were not marked by sharp and steady declines in net exports that ultimately resulted in their moving into negative territory. As Nakamura (1993, p. 167) explains this, "The current account of the balance of payments stopped being a constraint on economic growth under the exchange rate of

360 yen per dollar because international competitiveness had improved enough" (author's translation).

27. See the appendix at the end of this chapter for details on the construction of these series.

28. Such as Greece and Thailand in 1953, Iran in 1957, the Philippines in 1962, and India in 1966.

29. Kosai (1989).

30. Again, the difference is explicable by the tendency for other countries to devalue against the dollar and therefore the yen, which lowered foreign prices when converted into yen.

31. The figures here are abstracted from "Comparative Statistics" compiled by the Bank of Japan, following the classification in the *Monthly Bulletin of Statistics* of the United Nations. The UN's "Economic Class I" includes the United States, Canada, Belgium, Luxembourg, France, West Germany, Italy, the Netherlands, Austria, Denmark, Norway, Portugal, Sweden, Switzerland, the United Kingdom, Finland, Iceland, Ireland, Greece, Spain, Turkey, Yugoslavia, Japan, Australia, New Zealand, and South Africa. The figures for each country reflect changes in export prices on each national currency basis. The data series for "developed countries" is aggregated after adjusting each country's export price index for nominal exchange rates fluctuations against the dollar.

32. Shinohara (1959).

33. Kosai (1989, p. 287, authors' translation).

34. *Nikkei Newspaper*, 29 October 1958, author's translation. In the press, Erhard's comments were interpreted as implying that Japan should abolish its capital controls, the country's wage level is too low and should be raised, the exchange rate of 360 yen per dollar is undervalued and should be revalued, and Japan should expand domestic demand (see, for example, Hoshino 1958).

35. Bank of Japan (1986, p. 303). Angel (1991, p. 272) puts it more strongly, writing that "Expressions of doubt were banned absolutely within the MOF, and serious efforts were even made to prevent public discussion of the issue within the business community."

36. Cited in Japan Ministry of Finance (1992, p. 374, authors' translation).

37. The prominent exceptions were the members of the Forum for Foreign Exchange Rate Policy, who recommended revaluation and shifting to a crawling peg in their report issued on 10 July 1971. However, the members of the forum recommended limiting the yen's appreciation to 2 to 4 percent a year, reflecting widespread worries about the negative repercussions of a large step revaluation.

38. Bank of Japan (1986, p. 305). See also Takahashi (1971) and Hayami (1982).

39. The rise of trade tension with, inter alia, the United States, is another suggestive parallel between Japan in the 1970s and China today.

40. Takahashi (1971).

41. In June 1971. The relaxation of regulations included the liberalization of outward FDI in principle. The enhancement of liberalization of inward FDI was also in the list, reflecting the criticism from abroad on the slow pace of liberalization (Japan Ministry of Finance 1992, pp. 368–370).

42. Shimomura (1971).

43. In the Bank of Japan's retrospective analysis, the Japanese economy, which had begun to recover from the post-1969 recession in the summer of 1971, started to weaken again from the second half of August due to the effects of the so-called "Nixon shock" (Bank of Japan 1986, pp. 357–358).

44. Komiya and Suda (1983b, p. 41). It is interesting to note the parallels with Goldstein and Lardy's (2003) proposal for China for a two-step exit from the renminbi peg, the first step being a one-time revaluation against the dollar and the second step, after a period, being the transition to a managed float.

45. The allowance of open positions for authorized banks was reduced twice in the mid-1960s to discourage short-term capital outflows (Japan Ministry of Finance 1992, pp. 192–193).

46. Japan Ministry of Finance (1992, p. 212); Fukao (1990, pp. 119–121).

47. These ceilings were then transformed into limits on open positions in 1977 and abolished in 1984.

48. Fukao (1990, p. 24).

49. Those reserve requirements were then doubled in 1978.

50. See Ito (1986).

51. Even under the fixed exchange-rate system, interbank and customer exchange rates were allowed to fluctuate within narrow bands after the deregulation of 1959, encouraging transactions in the forward market to a certain extent. Prior to September 1959, the so-called MOF exchange rate, by which authorized foreign-exchange banks traded with the MOF, and customer exchange rates were fixed by decree of the finance minister. Deregulation allowed these rates to fluctuate between 0.5 percent above parity, 360 yen per dollar, and 0.5 percent below it (the band later expanded to 0.75 percent in 1963). At the same time, regulation of the forward exchange rate against the dollar was abandoned. (Forward rates against other currencies had been already deregulated.) Komiya and Suda (1983b, p. 23); Japan Ministry of Finance (1992, pp. 42–44).

52. Initially, the banks stopped quoting forward exchange rates for their customers, and trading volume on the interbank market collapsed.

53. Komiya and Suda (1983b, pp. 22–23).

54. Indeed, some controls were tightened or reimposed following the shift to managed floating, as noted. Revealingly, Fukao (1990) entitles a section of his paper "From 1973 to 1980: A Managed Float with Controls on Capital Movements."

55. Fujino (1988); Kosai (1989).

56. Miyagawa and Tokui (1994).

57. Miyagawa and Tokui (1994) use effective exchange rates provided by J. P. Morgan.

58. Other results are that global demand has a positive effect on investment, increases in the ratio of intermediate input prices to capital costs have a negative effect (as if capital and intermediate inputs are complements in production), and increases in the ratio of wages to capital costs have a positive effect (as if labor and capital are substitutes). Miyagawa and Tokui (1994) assume that trade industries are in a condition of monopolistic competition where appreciation of the national currency leads to worsening the competitiveness and thus results in decline in share of national industries in the global market.

59. Miyagawa and Tokui (1994).

60. Each variable is transformed into an index whose level in 1955 is 100. All data series are then expressed as logarithms.

61. The results of the Dickey-Fuller-GLS test, which is supposed to have enhanced power in small samples, show the same results.

62. Note that the real effective exchange rate here is defined as yen per unit of foreign currency.

63. As in Miyagawa and Tokui (1994).

64. Nakamura (1993).

65. All series are again transformed into logs prior to estimation.

66. Using both the augmented Dickey-Fuller and Dickey-Fuller-GLS tests.

67. Note that this is only one of many forms in which this relationship is estimated. Others have, for example, put the exchange rate on the left and domestic prices on the right and attempted to use it to track exchange-rate fluctuations. Since in this period the exchange rate was tightly managed, while domestic wholesale prices were free to move, it makes more sense to treat the exchange rate as exogenous and domestic prices as endogenous. And it is reasonable to assume that Japan was too small for its own inflation to significantly affect inflation in the rest-of-the-world aggregate.

68. Campa and Goldberg (2002).

69. Note that nominal effective exchange rates in the pre-1971 period fluctuated to some extent (for details, see the section on currency policy and figure 3.1).

70. Arguments stemming from the Lucas critique suggest that we might expect to find a higher pass-through coefficient in this later period insofar as floating made agents more aware of the possibility of exchange-rate fluctuations. In practice, this does not appear to be the case.

71. When a constant term is also included in the equation.

72. The actual appreciation on an annual average basis was 9.5 percent.

73. In 1971 and 1972, Japanese wholesale export prices declined by 3.2 percent, while wholesale prices rose by 1.6 percent, consistent with this distinction—and with the idea that Japanese exporters absorbed the

exchange-rate shock by cutting margins and thereby maintaining export market share. This response clearly varied by sector. The Economic White Paper of 1972 discusses the effects of yen's revaluation on the competitiveness of exporters and price-setting behavior of export sectors as follows (Economic Planning Agency 1972, pp. 70–71, authors' translation):

Looking at changes in export prices (on a foreign currency denominated basis) and export volumes in the period from the shift to a floating exchange rate system (in August 1971) to March in this year (1972), export volumes of electric machinery and transport equipment increased even though (foreign currency denominated) prices were raised enough to offset the impact of revaluation, reflecting strong competitiveness. The export volumes of steel and textiles fell due to the increase in export prices (on a foreign currency denominated basis) designed to partially absorb the effects of revaluation. . . . Some industries with weak competitiveness in the global market such as chemicals and foods were forced to keep export prices (on a foreign currency denominated basis) to maintain export volume.

74. See Eichengreen and Masson et al. (1998).

75. Blanchard and Giavazzi (2005).

76. The increase in the GDP deflator, which incorporates a lower weight on energy prices, rose from 6 percent in 1972 to 13 percent in 1973 and 21 percent in 1974.

Chapter 4

1. Persaud (2004, p. 1).

2. Here I am dissenting from one of Persaud's assertions.

3. See Wilson (1941) and Lindert (1969).

4. Gold coin constituted a large share of the circulation only in England, France, Germany, the United States, Russia after 1897, Australia, South Africa, and New Zealand, according to Bloomfield (1959).

5. See Redish (1990) and the author's other publications on this subject.

6. See Lindert (1969). They then rose further to roughly a quarter of global reserves in the 1920s, prompting observers to write, with

something of a lag relative to reality, of the emergence of a gold-exchange standard.

7. According to the estimates of Imlah (1958).

8. Williams (1968, p. 268).

9. Forward contracts in sterling traded in Liverpool from at least the 1850s.

10. On this, see Flandreau and Sussman (2005) and Bordo, Meissner, and Redish (2005). In the case of colonial and Commonwealth borrowers, the entire question of currency denomination was moot.

11. More so to the extent that they eventually were going to be used to purchase machinery, railway rolling stock, and other products of British industry.

12. See Balogh (1950), although it can be questioned, as Lindert does, whether it was the lender or the borrower whose behavior was most constrained by the practice.

13. See, for example, Crick (1948).

14. For example, Bloomfield (1959) notes that both the Bank of France and German Reichsbank, which oversaw the operation the main competing reserve centers, took various steps to make it difficult for market participants to export gold.

15. Persaud (2004, p. 1).

16. This is the analytical basis for formal models of international currency status. See, for example Matsuyama, Kiyotaki, and Matsui (1993).

17. To again quote Persaud (2004, p. 2), "Reserve currencies have the attributes of a natural monopoly or in more modern parlance, a network. If it costs extra to trade with someone who uses a different currency than you, it makes sense for you to use the currency that most other people use; this makes that currency yet bigger and cheaper to use. There is a good analogy with computers. 'Windows' is the dollar of operating systems."

18. See Krugman (1979). Chinn and Frankel (2005) provide the empirical analog to this argument.

19. Readers familiar with my own previous work on this subject (Eichengreen 1998) will notice that my views on this particular issue have evolved, as views sometimes do.

20. Lindert (1969, table 3). Note the qualification in the text: these cal-culations exclude from consideration the $232 million whose currency of denomination is not known.

21. Indeed, elevating its status in this way was one of the motivations for founding the Fed, according to Broz (1997).

22. This reflected the absence of a deep and liquid market in bankers' acceptances, which was itself a reflection of the fact that national banks were prohibited from accepting bills of exchange arising out of inter-national trade.

23. In 1914, it induced the New York banks to establish a gold pool for financing balance-of-payments settlements (note the parallel with the episode discussed in chapter 2). After the country entered the war, the government appealed to patriotism and erected various bureaucratic obstacles to discourage private gold exports. But fundamentally it was the strength of the U.S. balance of payments, given the country's sta-tus as a leading producer of manufactured exports and raw materials for the war effort, that allowed it to maintain convertibility in this dif-ficult period.

24. The beachhead effect (Baldwin 1988) refers to the lasting effects of U.S. penetration of foreign markets, notably in Latin America, in the period when Europe's trade was disrupted by war.

25. Sayers (1976, p. 211).

26. Triffin (1964) provides an estimate for 1928 of official reserves in dollars of $600 million, versus $2,560 million in other currencies. He estimates that reserves denominated in dollars then fell to $60 million at the end of 1933 with the collapse of the gold-exchange standard, while reserves denominated in other currencies fell to $1,055. Reserves in those other currencies may have been split seventy/thirty between sterling and the French franc, with a higher fraction probably being held in francs after 1931 when the convertibility of sterling into gold was suspended and the currency was allowed to float. See Nurkse (1944) and Bell (1956).

27. In fact, the raw data do not suggest that the dollar dominated the market for international reserves until the end of the 1950s. But the earlier period was one of significant disequilibrium: it was the years of the "dollar shortage," and the large sterling balances held by mem-bers of the Commonwealth and empire were blocked (that is, not held

voluntarily). Indeed, more than half of global foreign exchange reserves were held in sterling in 1949, and some 36 percent of reserves were held in this form in 1957. An indirect guide to the share of reserves that might have been held voluntarily was the share of the sterling area in global trade, which was about 30 percent in this period.

28. In addition, with the creation of the euro in 1999, French claims on Germany and German claims on France were effectively redenominated in the now common domestic currency and no longer counted as reserves, leading to a one-time decline in the share of foreign reserves denominated in European currencies.

29. Although, as noted by, inter alia, Schenk (2004), the colonies did possess a significant and growing amount of fiscal and financial autonomy after World War II and especially in the 1960s.

30. For discussion of this point, see Cohen (1971). Here the analogy with Asian currency policies in the current period is suggestive (see also chapter 1 above).

31. This is distinct from the ratio of total liquid liabilities to foreigners relative to total liquid assets held abroad, about which less is known and considerable controversy prevails (see Bloomfield 1963).

32. See chapter 1 above.

33. As argued by Dooley, Folkerts-Landau, and Garber (2004).

34. Despres, Kindleberger, and Salant (1966).

35. Salant (1966) provides a statement of the view that the tendency of the United States to borrow short and lend long reflected the lower costs and greater efficiency of financial intermediation in the United States. The language there is almost identical to the rhetoric used to characterize the differences between the U.S. and Chinese financial sectors today.

36. See Feis (1930), Lindert (1969), and Fishlow (1986).

37. Arguably, on these previous occasions the reserve-currency country was a net lender on *both* short- and long-term account (Bloomfield 1963). In the pre-1914 British case, for example, while the net short-term liabilities of the government and the central bank to their official foreign counterparts were positive, the net short-term liabilities of the country as a whole were probably negative, reflecting the large volume of private acceptance claims on foreigners (again, see Bloomfield 1963).

The same may have been true of France and Germany, although less is known about these cases.

38. Although prewar Britain ran a deficit on merchandise trade, net income from shipping, insurance, interest, and dividends was more than sufficient to produce a substantial current account surplus. The other side of this coin was a substantial capital outflow: between 1900 and 1913, Britain invested some 5 percent of its GDP abroad. The country's net foreign assets were on the order of a quarter of GDP. France invested perhaps 2 1/2 percent of its GDP abroad each year, and its net foreign asset ratio was perhaps half of Britain's. My own estimates (Eichengreen 2000a) suggest that the United States first became a net foreign creditor as a result of World War I, although the size of the net position was small. This is why contemporaries and historians were able to refer to the unparalleled pulling power of the Bank of England's discount rate. See, for example, Smit (1934). If foreigners began converting sterling reserves into gold—if Britain's liquid external liabilities and assets both began to fall—the country's long-term assets were easily liquefied. In particular, an increase in bank rate damped down, or at least delayed, long-term foreign lending. In addition, it encouraged overseas and foreign residents who were floating bonds in London to maintain a larger share of the proceeds on deposit there. Raising interest rates also raised interest earnings since the country was a net foreign creditor; that is, residents had more interest-earning assets abroad than foreigners maintained in Britain. It strengthened the balance of payments by contracting the volume of acceptances and other short-term claims on the rest of the world. The classic statement of this view is that of the Macmillan Committee (Committee on Finance and Industry 1931). Bloomfield (1963) provides a more agnostic approach to the question. On rare occasions, there was also the possibility of foreign support in the event that the Bank of England's liquid assets proved insufficient. For an earlier discussion of the same point, see Bloomfield (1959).

39. See Dooley and Garber (2005).

40. The phrase is from Summers (2004).

41. Mussa (2004).

42. Comparable rates of inflation between these two large markets are consistent with the long-run stability of exchange rates between them.

43. Or at least it stabilizes there under favorable assumptions. Note, for example, that I have said nothing about the increase in nominal interest rates that might accompany this higher inflation rate. Net interest payments to foreigners are part of the current account. If they rise with inflation, as is plausible, then the trade balance must strengthen to keep the current account from rising above 5 percent. (And if the term of the debt shortens in response to the acceleration of inflation, then the increase in interest liabilities becomes larger still, since the now-higher interest rate must be paid on a larger fraction of the outstanding debt.) If the trade balance doesn't strengthen, then the U.S. authorities have to respond with a further surprise increase in inflation, which elicits an increase in interest rates, and so forth in a vicious spiral. Presumably, this would render the dollar a still less attractive form in which to hold reserves.

44. The assumption that growth remains unchanged is a convenient simplification to which we may wish to return.

45. This is the classic portfolio-balance model of international adjustment, as in Kouri (1976) and updated by Blanchard, Giavazzi, and Sa (2005).

46. Here is where the assumption flagged in footnote 43 above should be relaxed.

47. A point emphasized by Tavlas (1997). If instead we assume that n must stabilize at 40 percent of U.S. GDP, Mussa's more conservative estimate of the feasible, then U.S. inflation must rise to 10.5 percent, more than five times foreign levels, which reinforces the conclusion.

48. A complication here is that depreciation of the dollar also has the effect of reducing the U.S. net external debt because U.S. foreign assets are disproportionately denominated in foreign currencies (as in the case, in some sense, of foreign direct investments) while U.S. foreign liabilities are disproportionately denominated in dollars (as emphasized by Gourinchas and Rey 2003 and Lane and Milesi-Ferretti 2004). But this too is likely to change in an environment of higher inflation and secular depreciation like that imagined in the text.

49. The possibility that sharp interest-rate increases that cause recession and financial distress could weaken the currency rather than strengthening it was much discussed in the aftermath of the Asian crisis. See, for example, Furman and Stiglitz (1998). The careful reader

will have noted that the first scenario has both inflation and currency depreciation accelerating, while the second has currency depreciation accelerating without a concurrent increase in inflation. The reason is that the real exchange rate has good reason to behave differently in the two scenarios; in the second one, real depreciation is required to begin crowding in the demand for U.S. goods.

50. This example is not entirely hypothetical. Rejection of the EU's draft constitution in the French and Dutch referenda in the spring of 2005 and dissatisfaction with slow economic growth led Italian welfare minister Roberto Maroni to suggest that Italy should consider leaving the single currency and reintroducing the lira. The possibility that the euro zone might dissolve was then reportedly discussed at a meeting of high-level German finance officials ("Italian Ministers" 2005; "Euro Plumbs 7½ Month Low" 2005).

51. A strong statement to the contrary is Blanchard (2004).

References

Ackley, Gardner, and Hiromitsu Ishi. (1976). "Fiscal, Monetary and Related Policies." In Hugh Patrick and Henry Rosovsky (Eds.), *Asia's New Giant* (pp. 154–247). Washington, DC: Brookings Institution.

Angel, Robert. (1991). *Explaining Economic Policy Failure: Japan in the 1969 1971 International Monetary Crisis*. New York: Columbia University Press.

Association of Public and Corporate Bond Underwriters (Koshasai Hikiuke Kyokai). (1980). *History of Public and Corporate Bond Market in Japan* (Nihon Koshasai Shijo Shi). Tokyo: Association of Public and Corporate Bond Underwriters.

Baldwin, Richard. (1988). "Hysteresis in Import Prices: The Beachhead Effect." *American Economic Review* 78, 773–785.

Balogh, Thomas. (1950). *Studies in Financial Organization*. Cambridge: Cambridge University Press.

Bank for International Settlements (BIS). (2005). *Seventy-fifth Annual Report*. Basel: BIS.

Bank of Japan. (various years). *Balance of Payments Monthly*. Tokyo: Bank of Japan.

Bank of Japan. (1987). *Hundred-Year Statistics of Wholesale Prices in Japan*. Tokyo: Bank of Japan.

Bank of Japan. (various years). *Price Indices Annual*. Tokyo: Bank of Japan.

Bank of Japan. (1985). *One-Hundred-Year History of the Bank of Japan* (Nihon Ginko Hyakunenshi). Vol. 5. Tokyo: Bank of Japan.

Bank of Japan. (1986). *One-Hundred-Year History of the Bank of Japan* (Nihon Ginko Hyakunenshi). Vol. 6. Tokyo: Bank of Japan.

Barro, Robert. (1979). "Money and the Price Level under the Gold Standard." *Economic Journal* 89, 13–33.

Bell, Philip. (1956). *The Sterling Area in the Postwar World.* Oxford: Clarendon Press.

Blanchard, Olivier. (2004). "The Economic Future of Europe." *Journal of Economic Perspectives* 18, 3–26.

Blanchard, Olivier, and Francesco Giavazzi. (2005). "China: A Three-Handed Approach." Manuscript, Massachusetts Institute of Technology, Cambridge, MA.

Blanchard, Olivier, Francesco Giavazzi, and Filipa Sa. (2005). "The U.S. Current Account and the Dollar." *Brookings Papers on Economic Activity* 1, 1–49.

Block, Fred L. (1977). *The Origins of International Economic Disorder: A Study of United States International Monetary Policy from World War II to the Present.* Berkeley: University of California Press.

Bloomfield, Arthur I. (1959). *Monetary Policy under the International Gold Standard 1880–1914.* New York: Federal Reserve Bank of New York.

Bloomfield, Arthur I. (1963). "Short-Term Capital Movements under the Pre-1914 Gold Standard." Princeton Studies in International Finance No. 11, International Finance Section, Department of Economics, Princeton University.

Bordo, Michael, and Barry Eichengreen. (1998). "Implications of the Great Depression for the Development of the International Monetary System." In Michael Bordo, Claudia Goldin, and Eugene White (Eds.), *The Defining Moment: The Great Depression and the American Economy in the Twentieth Century* (pp. 402–453). Chicago: University of Chicago Press.

Bordo, Michael, Christopher Meissner, and Angela Redish. (2005). "How Original Sin Was Overcome: The Evolution of External Debt Denominated in Domestic Currencies in the United States and the British Dominions." In Barry Eichengreen and Ricardo Hausmann

(Eds.), *Other People's Money: Debt Denomination and Financial Instability in Emerging Market Economies* (pp. 122–153). Chicago: University of Chicago Press.

Broz, Lawrence. (1997). *The International Origins of the Federal Reserve System.* Ithaca: Cornell University Press.

Campa, José Manuel, and Linda S. Goldberg. (2002). "Exchange Rate Pass-Through into Import Prices: A Macro or Micro Phenomenon?" NBER Working Paper No. 8934 (May).

Chinn, Menzie, and Jeffrey Frankel. (2005). "Will the Euro Eventually Surpass the Dollar as Leading International Reserve Currency?" NBER Working Paper No. 11510 (August).

Cohen, Benjamin J. (1971). *The Future of Sterling as an International Currency.* London: Macmillan.

Committee on Finance and Industry (Macmillan Committee). (1931). *Report.* London: HMSO.

Crick, W. F. (1948). *Origin and Development of the Sterling Area.* London: Institute of Bankers.

Despres, Emile, Charles Kindleberger, and Walter Salant. (1966). "The Dollar and World Liquidity: A Minority View." *The Economist* 218 (5 February), 526–529.

Dooley, Michael, David Folkerts-Landau, and Peter Garber. (2003). "An Essay on the Revived Bretton Woods System." NBER Working Paper No. 9971 (September).

Dooley, Michael, David Folkerts-Landau, and Peter Garber. (2004). "Direct Investment, Rising Real Wages and the Absorption of Excess Labor in the Periphery." NBER Working Paper No. 10,626 (July).

Dooley, Michael, and Peter Garber. (2005). "Is It 1958 or 1968? Three Notes on the Longevity of the Revived Bretton Woods System." *Brookings Papers on Economic Activity* 1, 147–187.

Economic Planning Agency. (1972). *Economic White Paper of 1972* (Showa 47 Nen-ban Keizai Hakusho). Tokyo: Printing Bureau of Ministry of Finance.

Eichengreen, Barry. (1992). *Golden Fetters: The Gold Standard and the Great Depression, 1919–1939.* Oxford: Oxford University Press.

Eichengreen, Barry. (1996a). *Globalizing Capital: A History of the International Monetary System*. Princeton: Princeton University Press.

Eichengreen, Barry. (1996b). "Institutions and Economic Growth: Europe after World War II." In Nicholas Crafts and Gianni Toniolo (Eds.), *Economic Growth in Europe since 1945* (pp. 38–72). Cambridge: Cambridge University Press.

Eichengreen, Barry. (1998). "The Euro as a Reserve Currency." *Journal of the Japanese and International Economies* 12, 483–506.

Eichengreen, Barry. (2000a). "From Benign Neglect to Malignant Preoccupation: U.S. Balance of Payments Policy in the 1960s." In George L. Perry and James Tobin (Eds.), *Economic Events, Ideas and Policies: The 1960s and After* (pp. 185–242). Washington, DC: Brookings Institution.

Eichengreen, Barry. (2000b). "U.S. Foreign Financial Relations in the Twentieth Century." In Stanley Engerman and Robert Gallman (Eds.), *The Cambridge Economic History of the United States*. Vol. 3, *The Twentieth Century* (pp. 463–504). Cambridge: Cambridge University Press.

Eichengreen, Barry. (2005). "Is a Change in the Renminbi Exchange Rate in China's Interest?" *Asian Economic Papers* 4, 40–75.

Eichengreen, Barry, and Paul Masson, et al. (1998). "Exit Strategies: Policy Options for Countries Seeking Greater Exchange-Rate Flexibility." Occasional Paper No. 168. Washington, DC: IMF (April).

Eichengreen, Barry, and Marc Uzan. (1993). "The 1933 World Economic Conference as an Instance of Failed International Cooperation." In Peter Evans, Harold K. Jacobson, and Robert D. Putnam (Eds.), *Double-Edged Diplomacy: International Bargaining and Domestic Politics* (pp. 171–206). Berkeley: University of California Press.

"Euro Plumbs Seven-and-a-Half-Month Low." (2005). Reuters, 1 June.

Feis, Herbert. (1930). *Europe, the World's Banker*. New Haven: Yale University Press.

Fishlow, Albert. (1986). "Lessons from the Past: Capital Markets during the Nineteenth Century and the Interwar Period." In Miles Kahler (Ed.), *The Politics of International Debt* (pp. 37–94). Ithaca: Cornell University Press.

Flandreau, Marc, and Nathan Sussman. (2005). "Old Sins: Exchange Clauses and European Foreign Lending in the Nineteenth Century." In Barry Eichengreen and Ricardo Hausmann (Eds.), *Other People's Money: Debt Denomination and Financial Instability in Emerging Market Economies* (pp. 154–189). Chicago: University of Chicago Press.

Flood, Robert, and Peter Garber. (1984). "Gold Monetization and Gold Discipline." *Journal of Political Economy* 92, 90–107.

Frankel, Jeffrey, and Katherine Rockett. (1988). "International Macroeconomic Policy Coordination When Policymakers Do Not Agree on the True Model." *American Economic Review* 78, 318–340.

Fujino, Shozaburo. (1988). "The Balance of Payments of Postwar Japan. Part One: Overvaluation of Exchange Rate of 360 Yen" (Sengo Nihon no Kokusai Shushi). *Keizai Kenkyu* 39, 97–108.

Fukao, Mitsuhiro. (1990). "Liberalization of Japan's Foreign Exchange Controls and Structural Changes in the Balance of Payments." *Bank of Japan Monetary and Economic Studies* 8, 1–65.

Furman, Jason, and Joseph Stiglitz. (1998). "Economic Crises: Evidence and Insights from East Asia." *Brookings Papers on Economic Activity* 2, 1–135.

Garber, Peter. (1993). "The Collapse of the Bretton Woods Fixed Exchange Rate System." In Michael Bordo and Barry Eichengreen (Eds.), *A Retrospective on the Bretton Woods System: Lessons for International Monetary Reform* (pp. 461–494). Chicago: University of Chicago Press.

Genberg, Hans, and Alexander Swoboda. (1993). "The Provision of Liquidity in the Bretton Woods System." In Michael Bordo and Barry Eichengreen (Eds.), *A Retrospective on the Bretton Woods System: Lessons for International Monetary Reform* (pp. 269–316). Chicago: University of Chicago Press.

Gilbert, Milton. (1968). "The Gold-Dollar System: Conditions of Equilibrium and the Price of Gold." Princeton Essays in International Finance No. 70, International Finance Section, Department of Economics, Princeton University.

"Gold Pool's First Years: Account Balanced." (1962). *Economist*, 29 December, pp. 1293–1294.

Goldstein, Morris, and Nicholas Lardy. (2003). "Two-Stage Currency Reform for China." *Asian Wall Street Journal*, 12 September, A9.

Gourinchas, Pierre-Olivier, and Hélène Rey. (2003). "International Financial Adjustment." Manuscript, University of California, Berkeley, and Princeton University, Princeton, NJ.

Gourinchas, Pierre-Olivier, and Hélène Rey. (2005). "From World Banker to World Venture Capitalist: U.S. External Adjustment and the Exorbitant Privilege." Manuscript, University of California, Berkeley, and Princeton University, Princeton, NJ.

Gowa, Joanne S. (1983). *Closing the Gold Window.* Ithaca: Cornell University Press.

Hayami, Masaru. (1982). *Ten Years' Experience with Floating: Voyage without a Chart* (Hendo Soba Sei 10 Nen: Kaizu naki Kokai). Tokyo: Toyo Keizai Shinpo Sha.

Henderson, Dale, and Stephen Salant. (1978). "Market Anticipations of Government Policies and the Price of Gold." *Journal of Political Economy* 86, 627–648.

Horiuchi, Akiyoshi. (1984). "Economic Growth and Financial Allocation in Postwar Japan." Brookings Discussion Paper in International Economics No. 18 (August).

Hoshino, Naoki. (1958). "The Intention of Mr. Erhard" (Eaharuto no Shin'i). *Daiyamondo*, 15 November.

Imlah, Albert. (1958). *Economic Elements in the Pax Britannica.* Cambridge, MA: Harvard University Press.

International Monetary Fund. (various years). *Annual Report.* Washington, DC: International Monetary Fund.

International Monetary Fund. (various years). *Balance of Payments Statistics.* Washington, DC: International Monetary Fund.

International Monetary Fund. (various years). *Direction of Trade Statistics.* Washington, DC: International Monetary Fund.

International Monetary Fund. (various years). *International Financial Statistics.* Washington, DC: International Monetary Fund.

"Italian Ministers Say Italy Should Study Leaving Euro." (2005). Reuters, 3 June.

Ito, Takatoshi. (1986). "Capital Controls and Covered Interest Parity between the Yen and the Dollar." *Economic Studies Quarterly* 37, 223–241.

Japan Economic and Social Research Institute, Cabinet Office. (n.d.). *Statistics Information Site.* <www.esri.cao.go.jp>.

Japan Ministry of Finance. (1976). *The Financial History of Japan: The Allied Occupation Period* (Showa Zaisei Shi). Vol. 3. Tokyo: Ministry of Finance.

Japan Ministry of Finance. (1977). *The Collected Data Series of Financial Statement Statistics of Corporations by Industry* (Hojin Kigyo Tokei Kiho Syuran). Tokyo: Economic and Social Research Institute (ESRI), Cabinet Office. Available at <http://www.esri.cao.go.jp>.

Japan Ministry of Finance. (1991a). *History of Financial and Monetary Policies in Japan, 1952–73: Finance: Monetary Policy and Financial System, Part I* (Showa Zaisei Shi). Vol. 9. Tokyo: Ministry of Finance.

Japan Ministry of Finance. (1991b). *History of Financial and Monetary Policies in Japan, 1952–73: Finance: Monetary Policy and Financial System, Part II* (Showa Zaisei Shi). Vol. 10. Tokyo: Ministry of Finance.

Japan Ministry of Finance. (1992). *History of Financial and Monetary Policies in Japan, 1952–73: International Finance and External Economic Affairs, Part II* (Showa Zaisei Shi). Vol. 12. Tokyo: Ministry of Finance.

Japan Ministry of Finance. (various years). *The Collected Data Series of Financial Statement Statistics of Corporations, by Industry.* Tokyo: Ministry of Finance.

Japan Ministry of Trade and Industry. (various years). *Annual Report of the Foreign Trade of Japan.* Tokyo: Ministry of Finance.

Keynes, John Maynard. (1944). "Speech to the House of Lords, May 23, 1944." In Donald Moggridge (Ed.), *The Collected Writings of John Maynard Keynes.* Vol. 26, *Activities, 1941–46: Shaping the Postwar World—Bretton Woods and Reparations* (pp. 9–21). London: Macmillan and Cambridge University Press.

Kojima, Kiyoshi (Ed.). (1972). *Structure and Development of Japanese Trade.* Tokyo: Shiseido.

Komiya, Ryutaro. (1988). *Current Japanese Economy: Macroeconomic Perspectives and International Economic Relations* (Gendai Nihon Keizai). Tokyo: University of Tokyo Press.

178 References

Komiya, Ryutaro, and Miyako Suda. (1983). *Contemporary International Finance: Theory, History and Policy* (Gendai Kokusai Kinyuron, Rekishi Seisaku-hen). Vol. 2, *History and Policy*. Tokyo: Nihon Keizai Shinbun Sha.

Kosai, Yutaka. (1989). "Economic Policy During the Era of High Growth." In Yasukichi Yasuba and Takenori Inoki (Eds.), *Economic History of Japan* (Kodo Seichoki no Keizai Seisaku). Vol. 8, *High Growth* (Nihon Keizaishi) (pp. 209–272). Tokyo: Iwanami Shoten.

Kouri, Pentti. (1976). "The Exchange Rate and the Balance of Payments in the Short Run and in the Long Run: A Monetary Approach." *Scandinavian Journal of Economics* 78, 280–304.

Krugman, Paul. (1979). "A Model of Balance of Payments Crises." *Journal of Money, Credit and Banking* 11, 311–325.

Lane, Philip, and Gian Maria Milesi-Ferretti. (2004). "Financial Globalization and Exchange Rate Changes." IMF Working Paper 05/03 (January).

Lindert, Peter H. (1969). "Key Currencies and Gold 1900–1913." Princeton Studies in International Finance No. 24, International Finance Section, Department of Economics, Princeton University.

Louchheim, Donald H. (1968). "Paris Boycotts Gold Pool of Eight Major Nations." *Washington Post*, 21 November, A12.

Maddison, Angus. (2001). *The World Economy: A Millennial Perspective*. Paris: OECD.

Mason, Mark. (1992). *American Multinationals and Japan*. Cambridge, MA: Harvard University Press.

Matsuyama, Kiminori, Nobuhiro Kiyotaki, and Akihiko Matsui. (1993). "Toward a Theory of International Currency." *Review of Economic Studies* 60, 283–307.

Meltzer, Allan H. (1966). "The Regulation of Bank Payments Abroad: Another Failure for the Government's Balance of Payments Program." In George P. Shultz and Robert Z. Aliber (Eds.), *Guidelines, Informal Controls, and the Market Place* (pp. 183–208). Chicago: University of Chicago Press.

Meltzer, Allan H. (1991). "U.S. Policy in the Bretton Woods Era." *Federal Reserve Bank of St. Louis Review* 73 (May/June), 54–83.

Mikuni, Akio, and R. Taggart Murphy (2002). *Japan's Policy Trap: Dollars, Deflation, and the Crisis of Japanese Finance*. Washington, DC: Brookings Institution.

Mitchell, Brian R. (1998a). *International Historical Statistics: The Americas 1750–1993*. Basingstoke: Palgrave Macmillan.

Mitchell, Brian R. (1998b). *International Historical Statistics: Europe 1750–1993*. Basingstoke: Palgrave Macmillan.

Mitchell, Brian R. (1998c). *International Historical Statistics: Africa, Asia and Oceania 1750–1993*. Basingstoke: Palgrave Macmillan.

Miwa, Ryoichi. (2003). "Postwar Democratization and Economic Reconstruction." In Takafusa Nakamura and Konosuke Odaka (Eds.), *Economic History of Japan*. Vol. 3, *A Dual Structure*. Oxford: Oxford University Press.

Miyagawa, Tsutomu, and Joji Tokui. (1994). *The Economics of a Strong Yen* (Endaka no Keizaigaku). Tokyo: Toyo Keizai Shinpo Sha.

Moon, Ihlwan. (2005). "A Great Place to Be a Bank: In South Korea, Profits Are Soaring from Smarter Consumer Lending." *Business Week* (7 November), 52.

Mussa, Michael. (2004). "Exchange Rate Adjustments Needed to Reduce Global Payments Imbalances." In C. Fred Bergsten and John Williamson (Eds.), *Dollar Adjustment: How Far? Against What?* (pp. 113–138). Washington, DC: Institute for International Economics.

Nakamura, Takafusa. (1993). *The Japanese Economy: Its Growth and Structure* (3rd ed.) (Nihon Keizai Shi: Sono Seicho to Kozo). Tokyo: University of Tokyo Press.

Nakamura, Takafusa. (2003). "The Age of Turbulence: 1937–54." In Takafusa Nakamura and Konosuke Odaka (Eds.), *Economic History of Japan*. Vol. 3, *A Dual Structure*. Oxford: Oxford University Press.

National Bureau of Statistics of China. (2001). *China Statistical Yearbook 2001*. Beijing: National Bureau of Statistics of China.

Nurkse, Ragnar. (1944). *International Currency Experience*. Geneva: League of Nations.

Odaka, Konosuke. (1989). "The Trace of Growth (2)" (Seicho no Kiseki [2]. In Yasukichi Yasuba and Takenori Inoki (Eds.), *Economic History of Japan* (Nihon Keizaishi). Vol. 8, *High Growth*. Tokyo: Iwanami Shoten.

Ohkawa, Kazushi, and Henry Rosovsky. (1973). *Japanese Economic Growth*. Stanford: Stanford University Press.

Ohkawa, Kazushi, Tsutomu Noda, Nobukiyo Takamatsu, Saburo Yamada, Minoru Kumazaki, Tuichi Shionoya, and Ryoshin Minami. (1967). *Estimates of Long-Term Economic Statistics of Japan since 1868*. Vol. 8, *Prices*. Tokyo: Toyo Keizai Shinposha.

Ohkawa, Kazushi, Nobukiyo Takamatsu, and Yuzo Yamamoto. (1974). *Estimates of Long-Term Economic Statistics of Japan since 1868*. Vol. 1, *National Income*. Tokyo: Toyo Keizai Shinposha.

Persaud, Avinash. (2004). "When Currency Empires Fall," 11 October, Available at <http://www.321gold.com/editorials>.

Redish, Angela. (1990). "The Evolution of the Gold Standard in England." *Journal of Economic History* 50, 789–805.

Roosa, Robert. (1967). *The Dollar and World Liquidity*. New York: Random House.

Salant, Walter S. (1966). "Capital Markets and the Balance of Payments of a Financial Center." In William Fellner, Fritz Machlup, and Robert Triffin (Eds.), *Maintaining and Restoring Balance in International Payments* (pp. 177–196). Princeton: Princeton University Press.

Sayers, Richard. (1976). *The Bank of England, 1891–1944*. Cambridge: Cambridge University Press.

Schenk, Catherine R. (2004). "The Empire Strikes Back: Hong Kong and the Decline of Sterling in the 1960s." *Economic History Review* 57, 551–580.

Servan-Schreiber, Jean Jacques. (1967). *Le Défi Américain*. Paris: Denoel.

Shimomura, Osamu. (1971). "Keeping the Parity Should Be the Principle of Economic Policy" (Heika Iji koso Keizai Seisaku no Kihon dearu). *Shukan Toyo Keizai* (special issue), 30 August, 43–52.

Shinohara, Miyohei. (1959). "Liberalization and Exchange Rate of 360 Yen" (Jiyuka to 360 Yen Reto). *Ekonomisuto*, 10 November, Reprinted in *Japan and the World Economy* (Sekai Keizai to Nihon) (pp. 22–30). Tokyo: Chikuma Shobo.

Shultz, George, and Kenneth Dam. (1977). *Economic Policy beyond the Headlines*. Stanford: Stanford Alumni Association.

Smit, Carel Jan. (1934). "The Pre-War Gold Standard." *Proceedings of the American Political Science Association* 16, 53–56.

Solomon, Robert. (1968). "A Two-Tier System: Permanent or Temporary?" Address to the Banking and Finance Seminar, Oklahoma State University, 18 November.

Solomon, Robert. (1977). *The International Monetary System 1945–1976*. New York: Harper & Row.

Summers, Lawrence. (2004). "The United States and the Global Adjustment Process." Third Annual Stavros S. Niarchos Lecture, Institute for International Economics, Washington, DC, 23 March.

Takahashi, Kamekichi. (1971). "Yen's Revaluation" (En Kiriage). *Mainichi Newspaper*, 4 May.

"Taking the Fun Out of Currency Speculation." (1964). *Business Week*, 14 March, pp. 132–133.

Tavlas, George. (1997). "The International Use of the U.S. Dollar: An Optimum Currency Area Perspective." *World Economy* 20, 709–747.

Toniolo, Gianni. (2005). *Central Bank Cooperation at the Bank for International Settlements, 1930–1973*. New York: Cambridge University Press.

Triffin, Robert. (1947). "National Central Banking and the International Economy." *Postwar Economic Studies* 7, 46–81.

Triffin, Robert. (1964). "The Evolution of the International Monetary System: Historical Reappraisal and Future Perspectives." Princeton Studies in International Finance No. 12, International Finance Section, Department of Economics, Princeton University.

Truman, Edwin M. (2005). "Comment on the Future of Central Bank Cooperation." Manuscript, Institute for International Economics, 20 June, available at <http://www.iie.com>.

U.S. Congress. (1982). *Report to the Congress of the Commission on the Role of Gold in the Domestic and International Monetary Systems*. Washington, DC: Government Printing Office.

U.S. President. (1984). *Economic Report of the President*. Washington, DC: Government Printing Office.

Williams, David. (1968). "The Evolution of the Sterling System." In C. R. Whitlesey and J. S. G. Wilson (Eds.), *Essays in Money and Banking in Honour of R.S. Sayers* (pp. 266–297). Oxford: Oxford University Press.

Wilson, Charles H. (1941). *Anglo-Dutch Commerce and Finance in the Eighteenth Century*. Cambridge: Cambridge University Press.

Yamazawa, Ippei, and Yuzo Yamamoto. (1978). *Estimates of Long-Term Economic Statistics of Japan since 1868*. Vol. 14, *Foreign Trade and Balance of Payments*. Tokyo: Toyo Keizai Shinposha.

Yasuba, Yasukichi, and Takenori Inoki. (1989). "An Overview: 1955–80." In Yasukichi Yasuba and Takenori Inoki (Eds.), *Economic History of Japan*, Vol. 8, *High Growth* (Gaisetsu, 1955–80 Nen, Nihon Keizaishi) (pp. 1–56). Tokyo: Iwanami Shoten.

Index